SAINT AUGUSTINE'S

ENCHIRIDION

SAINT AUGUSTINE'S
ENCHIRIDION

OR MANUAL TO LAURENTIUS
CONCERNING
FAITH, HOPE, AND CHARITY

Translated from
the Benedictine Text
with an Introduction and Notes

BY

ERNEST EVANS

D.D. Oxford, Hon. D.D. Glasgow,
Vicar of Hellifield, and
Canon of Bradford

LONDON
S · P · C · K
1953

First published in 1953
by S. P. C. K.
Northumberland Avenue, London, W.C.2

Printed in Great Britain by
Richard Clay and Company, Ltd., Bungay, Suffolk

CONTENTS

INTRODUCTION

Aurelius Augustinus was born in 354 at Thagaste in Numidia (now Sûk Aghas in Algeria). His father, Patricius, one of the poor gentry of the town, was a heathen, but became a Christian shortly before his death. His mother, St Monnica, was one of those Christian women who are the salvation of their husbands and their sons. Augustine was allowed to grow up unbaptized, though sufficiently acquainted with Christian ways of thought to feel at one critical moment of his life that even in the best of philosophical teaching there is but limited satisfaction, in the absence of the only saving name of Christ. His conversion, when it came, was only partly a conversion of mind—that had been vaguely and inaccurately Christian from his youth—but chiefly a conversion of will and character. Even in the ten years during which he was interested in Manichaeism the attraction of that religion was largely that it claimed to be a superior version of Christianity.

The story of his early life and his conversion, told by himself in his *Confessions*, is too well known to need repetition. When his student days were over, he became a professor of rhetoric (i.e. of what we should now call the faculties of arts and law) first at Carthage and afterwards at Rome and Milan. At Milan he heard the preaching of St Ambrose. Admiring at first the preacher's rhetorical skill, he soon came to appreciate the reasonableness of his instruction, discovering with some surprise that much that he had assumed to be authentic Christian doctrine was not the faith of the Church at all. After his conversion in 386, it was Ambrose who baptized him, on 25 April 387.

He now turned again to his own country. His father had died some years before; his mother died at Ostia as they were about to take ship for Africa. In Africa Augustine settled with a few companions to a kind of monastic life on an estate near his native town. In 391 a chance visit to the town of Hippo (now Bone on the coast east of Algiers) led to his detention there by the bishop Valerius, at the insistence of the people, in the office of presbyter. In 395, at the aged bishop's request, he was consecrated by the Primate of Numidia to be assistant and presumptive successor to Valerius. Valerius died soon afterwards, and Augustine became Bishop of Hippo, where he remained until his death in 430, living the communal life with his clergy, as he had formerly done with his friends.

In the *Life of Augustine*, written in 432, his friend and neighbour, Possidius, Bishop of Calama, says that " the works dictated and published by him are so many, and so many were his sermons, expositions, and discussions, given in church . . . that even one of those given to study would scarcely have time to read them all ".[1] Augustine himself, towards the end of his life, reviewed his published works, and in a volume called *Retractations* enumerated their titles, commented on passages which might have been, or had been, misunderstood, and made occasional corrections. Between 386 and 427 he had written ninety-three works, in two hundred and thirty-two books. The *Confessions* and the *Retractations* taken together are the father's own account of his life and activities.

Apart from his sermons and letters (which are, however, of great importance) the rest of St Augustine's works fall for

---

[1] In the Benedictine edition they extend to ten folio volumes: which speaks well for the industry of the medieval copyists, and for the zeal of the renaissance scholars who searched out and published these works.

the most part into four groups, as they deal with the central facts and doctrines of Christian theology or with one or other of the three controversies in which he was engaged. As the work before us, the *Enchiridion* or *Manual*, being a comprehensive statement of orthodox Christian teaching, touches at various points all four of these subjects, it will be well to consider them here, and to refer briefly to the questions involved in them.

(1)

We begin with two small but very valuable books, the *Sermon on the Creed*, addressed to catechumens, and the discourse *On the Faith and the Creed*, delivered by Augustine as a presbyter to an assembly of bishops in 393. Each of these is an outline sketch of Christian theology, in the form of a commentary on the Apostles' Creed in the version (slightly different from ours) then current in the African churches. Four books *On Christian Teaching*, begun in 397 and completed (after being laid aside for many years) only in 426, are a manual of instruction for those whose duty it is to interpret the Scriptures to the congregation. The first three books set out the principles on which Scripture is to be understood and its full meaning discovered: the fourth book is in itself a short treatise on the art of public exposition.

His greatest theological work is the fifteen books *On the Trinity*, begun in 398 and completed in 416, on which his own judgement is that they are unduly laborious " and I suspect that few can understand them ". They are in fact a most weighty and convincing elucidation and defence of the doctrine of the Holy Trinity, the first seven books expounding the doctrine on the basis of Holy Scripture, the last eight attempting the scientific justification of it. Part of the argument consists of an analogy between human nature as we know it by self-analysis, and the divine nature as we know it by revelation. It is of course impossible by inductive reasoning to prove anything regarding the existence and attributes of God: but, it being granted that, because he created us so, we are in his image, it is possible for us to observe in our own constitution certain trinities which serve as illustrations, rather than proofs, of what is revealed to us of the divine Trinity. The mind, with the knowledge by which it knows itself, and the love with which it loves itself: the memory, the understanding, and the will: these, and other like trinities, suggest the essential reasonableness of what is revealed to us of the Eternal.

St Augustine's most famous work, after the *Confessions*, is probably the twenty-two books *On the City of God*, begun in 416 and finished in 426, but published in parts as they were completed. Its immediate occasion was controversial. On the sack of Rome by the Vandals in 410 the old complaint was repeated that because the Empire had deserted the old gods who had made it great it was now abandoned by them to destruction by the barbarians. In books i–iv Augustine refutes this charge that Christianity is responsible for the sorrows of the world, and in books v–viii he discountenances the further claim made by the philosophers, that pagan religion is of value as a preparation for the life to come. In the remaining twelve books he sets out the history of the two polities, the city of God and the kingdom of this world, which are in this present age entwined and mingled together, the people of God being in exile in a strange land: yet the Church, the city of God come down from heaven, is as old as creation, a kingdom standing unshaken amid the crash of earthly empires, and to be made perfect in due time by restoration to its true and abiding home. Because of Augustine's habit (which the reader of the *Enchiridion* will not fail to notice) of pursuing casual phrases and suggestions with detailed discussion, the work appears to digress into byways only remotely connected with the main theme: yet the thread of the argument is invariably picked up again later, and the work as a whole presents a broadly sketched outline of Christian eschatology with a thorough discussion of many details. Probably no book ever written has had so powerful an effect as this on the religious and political thought of subsequent ages.

(2)

Large numbers of Augustine's works were written in controversy with Manichaeans, Donatists, and Pelagians. As the principles he opposed to theirs, and the conclusions he arrived at in the course of discussion, reappear in the work before us, it may be well to ascertain what were the questions at issue, and what answers Augustine gave.

The doctrines of the Manichaeans had great attraction for Augustine during that period of his life in which, as a young man of vigorous mind, he tended to be dissatisfied with the religion he had been vaguely and inconclusively taught in childhood. When at length, after many years of waiting, he succeeded in meeting a much-advertised Manichaean teacher named Faustus, the result was disappointing and the illusion vanished. He devoted much of the first ten years after his conversion to controversy against this superficially attractive, yet in many respects degrading, heresy.

Manes, or Manichaeus, the founder of the sect, was born in Babylon about 220. Asserting that he was the Paraclete promised by Christ, he taught a mixture of Persian and Christian doctrines with a general background of Indian pantheism. It is not always easy to distinguish his teaching from some forms of second-century gnosticism, which in fact had drawn upon the same sources. He was at first favourably treated by the Persian kings, but was eventually put to death at the instance of the magian priesthood. His

Fundamental Epistle was in the hands of Augustine, who wrote a reply to it. After his death, the sect became widely spread, from Turkestan to Morocco: the attractiveness of its doctrines is shown by their frequent resurgence (under other names) both in medieval and in modern times: and part of the danger was (and is) the claim that people can be Manichaeans and Christians at the same time.

Manichaeism, as already hinted, attempted to solve the problem of evil by reference to a Persian dualism upon a background of Indian pantheism: its terminology, along with some of its sacramental observances and its hierarchical organization, was borrowed from Christian sources. Persian dogma assumed the existence of two first principles, or two creators, one good and one evil. As both of these are indestructible there is, by this theory, a perpetual conflict between light and darkness, good and evil, life and matter; and the victory of the light, the life, the good, when it occurs, is not the destruction or subjection of their opposites, but only their own disentanglement from them. The final victory was envisaged as a gathering together of the elements of darkness and evil and matter into one mass or ball, and their isolation within a barrier constructed of such souls as had been unable to cleanse themselves of those adverse elements. Hence was deduced, for the elect (the highest grade in this religion), the need for asceticism in respect of material things: and, since it was regarded as undesirable to propagate life and thus imprison it in material bodies, there was some encouragement given to the practice of artificial birth-prevention. But the most mischievous thing was an inability to distinguish good and evil except in terms of spirit and matter, combined with the conviction that both of them have an equal right to exist: that is, the moral problem is shelved in favour of a metaphysical one, and this in turn is given up as insoluble. That is why Augustine found it impracticable to free himself from what he knew to be moral disorders, so long as he was under Manichaean influence: for if evil is a " thing in itself " (in Augustine's own terminology, a *natura*) it cannot be got rid of. It is this moral impotence of Manichaeism which explains his subsequent zeal against it.

But one cannot claim to have confuted dualism on this ground alone. One still has to explain how evil originated, and in what it consists. Augustine's thesis is that which is assumed rather than explicitly stated in both the Hebrew and the Christian Scriptures. It is, that there is one God, the almighty and good Creator of all things. He is not responsible for the existence of evil, for evil is not included among " all things ": " Evil as a thing in itself does not exist, but deprivation of goodness has acquired the name of evil." [1] When God made all things, he saw that they were very good: and part of that goodness was that to angels and men he had given freedom of the will, which is at the summit of his good gifts. Necessarily so: for without it the rational creation would not have been able to render to God the service of living agents, but only of animate machines. Lucifer, the angel of light, along with certain angels, his partisans, misused his freedom to set himself in opposition to his Creator, lost his goodness, and became Satan: and men likewise, from Adam downwards, have misused their freedom and thus become alienated from God. This, then, is the origin of evil, and its nature: it is a negation, due to disobedience to the will of God, and to declension from primal goodness: and the measure of the declension is the measure of the evil. Even so, nothing exists that is entirely and utterly evil: for since existence is goodness, to decline from goodness is to decline from existence, and to become totally devoid of goodness would be to cease to exist.

We cannot complain if there are some to whom Augustine's

[1] Cf., e.g., *Confessions* iii. 7.

explanation seems specious rather than convincing. We
cannot shut our eyes to certain physical evils in the world,
which have no demonstrable connexion with human sin.
Augustine would no doubt have explained them as due to the
malignant action of the revolted angels: we should be
inclined to regard them as the growing pains of mundane
evolution. But his theory has at least this advantage, that it
expounds the moral problem as a moral problem, neither
shelving it in favour of transcendental physics, nor making its
solution impossible by making evil eternal. Augustine's own
summary of his position is that there is no evil at all except sin
and those consequences which are the penalty of sin: *hoc est
totum quod dicitur malum, peccatum et poena peccati*.[1] And he
would add that those cosmic evils, for which man is not responsible, have in any case no relevancy to our attainment
to eternal life.[2]

(3)

Donatism is referred to in the *Enchiridion* only briefly and in
passing. It was a schism rather than a heresy, though Donatists did in practice ally themselves both with heretics and
with criminals, for the affliction of the Church which they
hated.

For its origins, in the early years of the fourth century,
and for the attempts at conciliation in which Augustine took
a leading part, the church histories should be consulted. The
questions at issue in the controversy were stated by Optatus
of Mileve (*circa* A.D. 370) somewhat as follows:

(1) Whether, as a matter of historical fact, Felix of Aptunga
and others concerned in the consecration of Caecilian, Bishop
of Carthage, had been traditors, i.e. had surrendered the

[1] *De Vera Religione* 12.
[2] See on this subject T. A. Lacey, *Nature, Miracle, and Sin:
A Study of St Augustine's Conception of the Natural Order.*

church books during the persecution and had thus committed a sin equivalent to apostasy. The Donatists affirmed that they had: the imperial commissioners appointed by Constantine had declared the charge unfounded.

(2) Whether the postulate of the holiness of the Church involves the perpetual exclusion from it of all who have sinned, especially those who have sinned by apostasy. The Donatists affirmed this, and added that a Church which granted reconciliation to such sinners immediately ceased to be a Church. The Catholics referred to the Parables of the Tares and of the Drag-net, which seem intended to meet precisely such a situation with a warning against rash disciplinary action.

(3) Whether, if any particular minister of the Church is a sinner, all his ecclesiastical acts are thereby made invalid. Here it is assumed by both parties that without the sacraments of baptism and the eucharist, and the valid orders which ensure their due administration, there is no assurance of salvation. The Donatists alleged that the sin of Felix of Aptunga (on which they insisted in spite of denials) invalidated the consecration of Caecilian and all his successors, and of all bishops and presbyters who associated with him or with them. The Catholics replied that in that case, seeing that all men are sinners, and that God alone knows men's hearts, there are no valid sacraments at all; but that in fact our Lord himself is in his own Person the minister of every sacrament, using as his agent the Christian minister for the time being, and that consequently the sin of any minister does not deprive of the grace of Christ such as in good faith avail themselves of his ministrations.

(4) Whether the practice of receiving again into communion sinners who have repented defiles the Church's holiness, causes it to cease to be the Church, and invalidates all baptisms administered by it. The Donatists affirmed this,

B

and were accustomed to baptize afresh persons whom they persuaded to leave the Catholic Church and join their body.

(5) The Donatists were in the habit of destroying catholic churches, pulling down their altars, defiling the sacred vessels, and trampling on the holy sacrament, as well as waylaying, with assault and murder, catholic bishops and presbyters. They denied the sacredness of these persons and things, on the ground that they had no connexion with their own " one true church ". It is to violence of this kind that Augustine refers in the book before us: he was, in fact, being so successful in persuading many to end the schism, that the irreconcilables were the more incensed against him.

Apart from the points already mentioned, or in summary of them, the Donatist schism raises the question whether the Church is to be a small company of the morally perfect living in isolation from the world, or whether it is to retain as its members those who make no claim to be either perfect or sinless. Moreover, looked at squarely, Donatism claims to make one man's salvation dependent upon another man's faith or morals: Pelagianism, the next heresy to be noticed, makes each man's salvation depend upon his own morals, rather than upon the saving grace of Christ through faith.

(4)

The doctrines of the Fall, of Sin both original and actual, of Predestination and Election, of Redemption through Christ alone, and of Grace both prevenient and concomitant, which Augustine maintained, and to some extent developed, in controversy with Pelagians, recur again and again throughout the *Enchiridion*. They were in no sense new doctrines, nor were they in themselves controversial. They are expounded or assumed in the Epistles of St Paul, and in many other places of the New Testament. The novelty was the Pelagian denial or slurring over of them.

For the details of the controversy as it occupied the last twenty years of Augustine's life (and was continued intermittently for a hundred years after his death, until the Council of Orange in 529) the reader must again be referred to the church histories. The questions at issue can only be briefly stated.

Both parties were agreed that it was necessary to do justice to three sets of premises, the doctines contained in or to be deduced from Holy Scripture, those formulated in the Creed or expounded by the great theologians, and those implied in the Church's sacramental system and penitential practice. From the Scriptures we derive the most comprehensive of all major premises, that God is the only creator and ruler and sustainer of the world, and that having made all things he saw that they were very good. Yet as the existence of evil cannot be denied, it is accounted for as the act, or the inevitable consequences of the act, of angelic and human wills which God created good and therefore free, but which have misused their freedom to oppose or thwart God's purpose. The first recorded human sin is that of Adam. The church fathers derived from St Paul the doctrine that the consequences of Adam's sin were passed on to all his descendants, not by imitation only, but because the corruption of nature caused by sin is communicated from parents to children at every act of generation. Likewise the fathers maintained, still following (as they thought) St Paul, that one of the consequences of sin is death : and they added (as St Paul does not) that but for sin Adam would not have died.

The Pelagians denied that (except by imitation) Adam's sin affected anyone but himself. They shut their eyes to that warp or eccentricity of human nature by which it finds the downward moral path easier than the upward. Of this warp or corruption Augustine (and not he alone) was deeply conscious. In forthright language he describes fallen human nature as a "mass of perdition".[1]   In spite of Scripture[2] and his own better knowledge, he can hardly disabuse his mind of the idea that the act of procreation (even within lawful marriage) is in some sense a sinful act—if only in that it results in the perpetuation of a sinful nature.

Thus we come to a distinction, which is often implied in the fathers' language, but which Augustine puts into words, between "first nature", which is human nature as God created it, and "second nature", which is that nature as corrupted by sin. Also we are led to state that fallen human nature, in so far as it is fallen, is in some sense distasteful to God : that is to say, that sin involves guilt, and merits the wrath of God. Consequently, in any discussion of the Atonement, we must take account of two factors, removal of the guilt by repentance and restoration to divine favour, and the rehabilitation and redintegration of human nature out of corruption into that first nature in which God created it. Both of these, according to Augustine and all the church fathers, are an act of divine grace given through Christ : if we are to distinguish, the former is mediated through faith in Christ crucified, while the latter, being "the power of his resurrection", is effected by the Holy Spirit in the Church through the sacraments. In any case, it is "of grace", the free and unmerited gift of God in Christ, and the two processes are concurrent and not really distinguishable.

In Greek and in Latin the term "grace" has the same variety of meanings as it has in English. Apart from ideas like "beauty" or "thankfulness", which are only in second instance germane to our present subject, there is always

---

[1] This expression, however, is not as strong as it sounds. "Mass" means the dough in the kneading-trough, and the "perdition" or destructive influence is envisaged as working in it like leaven.

[2] E.g. Hebrews 13. 4, which is a statement (A.V.), not a command (R.V.).

involved some association with the kindred word *gratis*,
" given freely and without price ".   So the grace of God is
that outpouring of God's mercy and loving-kindness which,
unable to rest in mere kindly regard, issues in actual help
given through Christ and made operative by the Holy Spirit.
The Pelagians tended to regard divine grace as given chiefly
or even exclusively in commandments and precepts.   They
claimed that when a man knows what he ought to do, he has
in himself complete power to accomplish it.   The church
teachers, from the apostles downwards, were more deeply
conscious of man's incapacity.   They saw that what was
needed was not only the informing of the mind but the
guidance and strengthening of the will.   To them the grace
of God was that actual help by which the human will is so
fortified and directed that the love of God becomes, so to
speak, an effective power without which no good act is possible, and with which no degree of sanctity is inconceivable.
And they claimed that this grace is just as essential to the
inception of a work of righteousness as it is to its accom-
plishment.

So far Augustine says nothing that has not frequently been
said before.   But now a further question arises.   If God's
grace is what we have claimed that it is, his actual help given
through Christ for the restoration of man to that first nature
from which he has fallen, and if God is almighty, must we
conclude that grace is irresistible?   Must we say that the grace
of God, the effectual working of his Holy Spirit, not only
strengthens man's will but also guides and directs it without
possibility of misunderstanding or failure?   If so, what has
become of that freedom of the will which was one of our first
postulates?   These were aspects of the question which
hitherto had hardly been discussed, and it is possible that
Augustine, with his strong consciousness and conviction of
the power of God's grace, was induced, by opposition to

Pelagian denials, to minimize or explain away the evident facts of human freedom and responsibility, all the while claiming (by subtleties of reasoning) to be maintaining them both unimpaired.

A further set of questions arose from the consideration of texts like Romans 8. 29 ("whom he did foreknow etc.") and 1 Peter 1. 2 ("elect according to the foreknowledge of God the Father"): though no doubt they would have arisen in any case as soon as the implications of certain theological postulates were followed up. If God is omniscient, it was at least within his power to know, before ever the world began, all things down to the last detail which ever were to be done in it. Must we then suppose that he did from all eternity know all that was ever to happen, including the names and the details of the character of all who were to be saved and all who were to perish? If so, even apart from the question of his omnipotent will, does not this imply that all events and actions are determined beforehand, no room being left for any human freedom of choice? And if it is the case that God knew, before the foundation of the world, that such and such persons would be brought through Christ to eternal life, while others would remain in sin and death, does not this involve the election of some and the rejection of others? In that case where is God's righteousness? And, in the long run, what need was there for the Incarnation and the Atonement, or for any divine act in the world, to effect what was determined upon already and could have been accomplished by a mere fiat? If St Augustine's solution of these problems, summarized in the *Enchiridion*, and worked out in detail elsewhere, seems more confidently expressed than persuasive, and dangerously like special pleading, he must at least receive the credit of having squarely faced the facts. These problems are not peculiar to theology, far less to Augustine's special treatment of it: they are among the most exacting problems of metaphysics—unless indeed we allow ourselves to be satisfied with a Democritean cosmogony and behaviourist morals.

Both parties to this controversy accepted at its face value the scriptural narrative of creation and the fall, and agreed that the whole human race is descended from two first parents whom God had created perfect and sinless. There is therefore, to the modern mind, a certain unreality in these discussions. No competent anthropologist, it appears, would now admit that the whole race is descended from two parents, or that we were ever in a condition such as could be described as "original righteousness": nor would it be admitted that anything ever happened, as a fact of primeval history, which could be rightly described as a "fall". The assumption would rather be that humanity has been, on the whole though not continuously, stepping upwards, from beast to man, from savagery to civilization, and that human history is a history of progress. Can we in such a context maintain our doctrine of the Fall and of Original Sin? Without necessarily assenting to every detail of the theories of the anthropologists, we might perhaps point out that, on our own admission, human nature is not what we know it ought to be, adding the suggestion that even in its progress upwards it has suffered from a kind of warp or declension towards evil: man is not, man has never at any stage succeeded in being, what God at that stage intended him to be: his progress may have been continuous, but it has been crooked: and this crookedness has produced a "second nature" in spiritual things, which only the grace of Christ can restore to that "first nature" into which it was God's purpose that man should develop. Pelagianism is very flattering to man's self-esteem: but Augustine should have the credit of not having shut his eyes to unpleasant facts.

The *Enchiridion* (this Greek word was apparently current in

Latin for " manual " or " handbook ") was written in 421 at
the request of Laurentius, a Roman layman, who had asked for
a short treatise on Christian faith and practice. It is the only
work of St Augustine which treats of the Christian life as a
whole. Probably some of the subjects discussed in detail will
seem to go beyond what is strictly necessary in a book on
essential things. It would appear, however, that besides being
the outcome of a fertile mind and of an honesty of purpose
which never shirks an awkward question, the digressions
which diversify without breaking the argument are really
concerned with matters which were then under discussion and
with problems which were capable of troubling those
unlearned in systematic theology. The proposed subject of
the book is faith, hope, and charity, and its argument is
developed under those heads. The faith is faith in man's
redemption through Christ, as professed in summary form in
the Creed. The hope is, for Christians themselves, of the
resurrection of the dead, of perfect peace, and of eternal
felicity : and, more generally, of the restoration to its pristine
integrity of that city of God which is eternal in the heavens.
Charity is that love of God which is poured forth in our
hearts by the Holy Spirit who is God's special gift in Christ :
and it is exercised in love for God, and in prayer to him,
combined with prayer for and well-doing towards one's
neighbour. Hence the treatise contains, among much else, a
discussion of the outstanding articles of the Creed, an outline
of Christian duty, and an analysis of the Lord's Prayer. It
contains very little reference to the details of the administration of the sacraments, though the importance of these
(especially baptism) is recognized : probably St Augustine,
like most of the fathers, thought these ought to be made use of
rather than talked about : and in any case, no one at that
period had any doubt of their value.

The book begins with an introduction addressed personally

to Laurentius.   Man's wisdom is piety, which is the service of God.   God is to be served by faith, hope, and charity, and the essence of these is comprised in the Creed and the Lord's Prayer (§§ 1–8).   So the main body of the work is an exposition of the Faith, following the order of the Creed, but with digressions or expansions on various subsidiary questions as they arise (§§ 9–113).

The main principle, that God is the Creator of all things, suggests the question of the origin of evil, and various problems dependent on this: namely, the nature of error and deception, and its gravity; sin and its penalty; God's purpose for mankind, and its fulfilment through salvation by the faith of Christ, by the operation of God who alone is able both to will and to perform; and the need for a Mediator who shall save from the wrath of God (§§ 9–33).

Concerning Christ the Mediator, the exposition begins with the fact of his virginal conception and birth, the assurance that he is both God and Man, and a discussion of the meaning of the expression of the Creed, "conceived by the Holy Ghost", and of the scriptural statement that he was made to be sin for us.   This leads to the consideration of the sacrament of baptism and the nature and extent of the sin remitted through it, together with its character as a death unto sin and a new birth unto righteousness.   Returning to the Creed, we observe that the redemptive act of Christ, in his death, his burial, his resurrection and ascension, is a figure of the Christian life: and we touch briefly upon the nature of the judgement to come (§§ 34–55).

On the third paragraph of the Creed, concerning the Holy Spirit and the Church, we consider the heavenly Church, which consists of the holy angels, and various questions relating to them: Christians look for the restoration of all things in Christ, and for the peace of God which passeth all understanding (§§ 56–63).

A long section on the remission of sins raises the question of the effect of present penance on future purgation, the benefit acquired after death through present alms and oblations, and the utility of prayer for the forgiveness of venial sin. For the forgiveness of one's own sins there is need of almsgiving, as well as the forgiveness of others, for by this means almsgiving is done to oneself. A distinction is suggested between grave and light sins, and it is emphasized that all sins are grave beyond repair except for the undeserved mercy of God (§§ 64–83).

On the resurrection of the flesh, questions arise touching the future state of abortions and monstrosities, the fundamental principle being that the whole flesh will be restored in its integrity and in complete seemliness. We discuss the nature of " spiritual bodies ", and the purpose of the resurrection of the damned. Final felicity will bring complete knowledge and reassurance concerning the righteousness of God : and thus we are led to consider the question of predestination, the meaning of " will have all men to be saved ", the invincible will of God, and the bearing of predestination and divine foreknowledge on the freedom of the human will, together with the overriding necessity of God's grace. Finally we take note of the intermediate state of waiting for the resurrection, and the utility of prayers, alms, and oblations for the dead. Christians look for the eternal felicity of the city of God, but do not forget the eternal punishment of those who are righteously excluded from it (§§ 84–113).

A brief discussion of hope and charity includes an analysis of the Lord's Prayer, a synopsis of the four stages of approach to Christian perfection, and a commendation of charity as the sum of all the commandments (§§ 114–121). A final note commends the book to its recipient (§ 122).

The present translation is made from the Benedictine folio

edition, Antwerp, 1701. This was reissued in a handy
reprint by C. H. Bruder, Leipzig, 1870, who contributed
nothing new except a few gratuitous misprints and mis-
punctuations.   For the benefit of those who wish to consult
the Latin text, these are corrected in the notes to this translation.   The smaller chapter divisions are given for con-
venience of reference: the longer divisions of the Benedictine
edition are added (in Roman numerals) as indicating better the
grouping of the subject matter.   Words and sentences
enclosed in square brackets are absent from some of the manuscripts: some of them are manifest interpolations.   The
chapter-headings are not part of the text: they are the
translator's abbreviations of those printed in the Benedictine
margin.   Quotations from Holy Scripture follow as closely
as possible the phraseology of the standard English versions:
variations are introduced when St Augustine's Latin text
suggests some significant difference of meaning.

ST AUGUSTINE'S
MANUAL TO LAURENTIUS
CONCERNING FAITH, HOPE, AND CHARITY

THE GIFT OF TRUE WISDOM

1. There are no words to express, my dear son Laurentius, I my great delight in your learning, and my great desire for you to be wise—not one of those to whom applies, *Where is the wise, where is the scribe, where is the disputer of this world? Hath not God made foolish the wisdom of this world?*,[1] but one 5 of those of whom it was said, *The multitude of the wise is the health of the world*,[2] and such as the apostle desires those to be to whom he says, *But I would have you to be wise indeed in that which is good, but simple in that which is evil.*[3] [For just as none can cause himself to exist, so also no one can cause him-10 self to be wise: this is possible only by illumination from him of whom it is written, *All wisdom is from God.*[4]]

PIETY, THE SERVICE OF GOD

2. Now the wisdom of man is piety. This you will find in the book of Saint Job. For there we read what wisdom herself has said to man, *Behold, piety is wisdom.*[5] If, however, you ask what is meant by piety in that context, you will find it more precisely in the Greek, *theosebia*, the worship of 5 God. For piety in Greek is also expressed by another word, *eusebia*, " good worship ", though this also has primary reference to worshipping God. But nothing is more satisfactory than the other word, for by it, in the explanation of what

[1] 1 Cor. 1. 20.   [2] Wisd. 6. 24.   [3] Rom. 16. 19.
[4] Ecclus. 1. 1.   [5] Job 28. 28.

1

10 man's wisdom is, the worship of God is expressly mentioned.
Are you looking for any shorter expression than this, when
you ask of me a short statement of great matters? Or is it
perhaps this very question that you desire to have shortly
expounded and summarized in a short discourse—how ought
15 God to be worshipped?

GOD IS SERVED BY FAITH, HOPE, AND CHARITY

3. If at this point I answer that God ought to be worshipped by faith, hope, and charity, you will at once object
that this is expressed more briefly than you wish; and you
will next ask for a brief explanation of the things which
5 appertain to each one of these three—what in fact must be
believed, what hoped for, and what loved. When I have
done this, there you will have all those things which you set
down in your letter by way of question. If you have a
copy of it by you, it is easy for you to turn them up and
10 read them over: if you have no copy, then recollect them
as I advert to them.

THE QUESTIONS PROPOSED

4. Your wish is, you write, for me to make a book which
you may have as a manual (as they call it), so that it may
never be out of your hands, a book which includes the things
requisite—that is, what is chiefly to be followed; what, in
5 view especially of divers heresies, is to be avoided; to what
extent reason argues in favour of religion, or what it is, when
there is faith alone, that does not come under reason; what
is held as primary, what as ultimate; what is the sum total
of the whole of what is laid down; and what is the unassail-
10 able and particular foundation of the catholic faith. Now
all these things which you are looking for you will without
doubt obtain knowledge of by diligently taking cognizance

of what ought to be the content of faith, the object of hope, and the object of love. For these especially, yea rather these only, are to be followed in religion. He who speaks 15 against these is either totally alien from the name of Christ, or else a heretic. These are the things to be defended by reason, either such reason as takes its rise from the perceptions of the body, or such as is discovered by the intelligence of the mind. Such matters, however, as we have neither experi- 20 enced by corporal perception nor have been nor are able to attain to with the mind, are without any hesitation to be believed on the testimony of those by whom has been compiled that which has long ago earned the name of divine Scripture: for these men, whether by means of their body 25 or by means of their mental faculties, have by divine assistance had the power either to see or even to foresee them.

THE ONE FOUNDATION

5. Now when the mind has been initiated in the beginnings of that faith which worketh by affection,[1] it makes it its purpose by well living even to attain to sight, wherein has been made known to holy and perfect hearts that ineffable beauty the full vision of which is supreme felicity. This in 5 fact is the object of your quest, what it is that is held as primary, what as ultimate—to be begun in faith, to be made perfect in sight. This also is the sum total of the whole of what is laid down. But the unassailable and particular foundation of the catholic faith is Christ himself. For, says 10 the apostle, *Other foundation can no man lay except that which is laid, which is Christ Jesus.*[2] Nor is there any need to deny that this is the particular foundation of the catholic faith, on the ground that it can be supposed that it is common to us and certain heretics. For if we give careful consideration to 15

[1] Gal. 5. 6.   [2] 1 Cor. 3. 11.

the things which pertain to Christ, it is in name and no more
that Christ is found among any heretics at all who wish to
have the designation of Christians : whereas in fact he is not
among them. But to prove this would take too long, for
20 we should have to enumerate all the heresies, either which
have existed or which do exist or which could have existed
under the Christian name, and to show the truth of our
statement in respect of them all one by one. And this
discussion would take so many volumes that it would seem
25 there is no end to it.

THE PURPOSE OF A MANUAL

6. You, however, are asking of me a manual, that is, something that can be held in your hands, not something to load
your bookcases. So, to return to those three means by which
I said God should be worshipped, faith, hope, and charity,
5 it is easy enough to state what is the content of faith, the
object of hope, and the object of charity : but the manner in
which this is defended against the cavils of those who hold
opposing views is a matter of more laborious and extensive
instruction : and to possess this it is not the hand that needs
10 to be filled with a short manual, but the heart that must be
inflamed with great zeal.

THE CREED AND THE LORD'S PRAYER

II   7. For you have in your possession the Creed and the
Lord's Prayer. What more brief than these does one hear
or read? What more easily does one commit to memory?
For in that by reason of sin the human race was oppressed
5 with great misery, and stood in need of divine mercy, the
prophet, foretelling of the time of God's grace, said, *And it
shall be, that everyone that calleth on the name of the Lord shall be*

saved.[1] This is the reason for the [Lord's] Prayer. But when the apostle, for the commendation of that grace, had quoted this prophetic testimony, he at once added, *But how shall they call on him in whom they have not believed?*[2] This is the reason for the Creed. In these two you can see you have those three: faith believes; hope and charity pray. Yet without faith the other two cannot exist: and consequently faith also prays. That in fact is why it was said, *How shall they call on him in whom they have not believed?*

FAITH, HOPE, AND LOVE ARE INSEPARABLE

8. Now what can one hope for if one does not believe it? —although there is even something not hoped for which yet can be an object of belief. For which of the faithful does not believe the punishments of the ungodly, and that without hoping for them? And any man who believes that they threaten him, and with an evasive motion of mind shrinks from them, is more correctly said to fear than to hope. A certain poet distinguishes between them, saying

> At least let hope remain to him that fears:[3]

though another poet, a far greater one, has used the word in no true sense,

> If e'er I could have hoped such grief as this.[4]

In fact some writers on the art of composition use this word as an instance to illustrate imprecise expression, and comment: " She said hope instead of fear." Thus there is faith both of evil things and of good, because both good things and evil are an object of belief, and that by good faith, not by bad. There is also faith both of things past and of things present and future. For we believe that Christ died, which is now past: we believe he sits at the right hand of the

[1] Joel 2. 32; Rom. 10. 13.   [2] Rom. 10. 14.
[3] Lucan, *Pharsalia* 2. 15.   [4] Virgil, *Aeneid* 4. 419.

C

Father, which now is: we believe he shall come to judge [the quick and the dead], which is to be. Also there is faith of one's own affairs and of others'. For each person believes that he once began to exist and that consequently he did not
25 exist from everlasting: and the same of other men, and other things. And not only of other men do we believe many things which pertain to religion, but also of the angels. Hope, however, is concerned only with good things, with things future, with things pertaining to the one who purports
30 to have the hope of them. And that being so, for these reasons faith must be distinguished from hope, as in verbal expression so also in rational qualification. For that which is concerned with not seeing, whether it be the objects of belief or the objects of hope, is common to faith and hope.
35 Indeed in the Epistle to the Hebrews, which notable defenders of the catholic creed have used as evidence, faith is said to be *conviction concerning things not seen* [1]—although whenever one professes he has believed, that is, has applied faith to, neither words nor witnesses nor indeed any proofs, but the
40 evidence of present facts, he does not seem to be so far astray as to be with justice rebuked for the expression and to be told, " You have seen it, and therefore have not believed ". From which one may suppose that it does not follow that there can be no sight of anything which is an object of faith.
45 Yet we do better to use the term " faith " of that which the divine pronouncements have taught us to call by that name, that in fact whose object is the things not seen. Concerning hope also the apostle says, *Hope which is seen is not hope: for what one seeth, why doth he hope for? But if we hope for that*
50 *we see not, we do through patience look out for it.* [2] When then good things are believed to be in store for us they are rightly said to be hoped for. And now what shall I say of love, without which faith is unprofitable? But hope cannot exist

[1] Heb. 11. 1.   [2] Rom. 8. 24, 25.

without love. In fact, as says the apostle James, *Even the devils believe, and tremble* : [1] yet they neither hope nor love, 55 but rather, while believing that that is to come which we hope for and love, they are in fear. For which reason the apostle Paul gives approval and commendation to the faith which works through affection ; [2] and certainly without hope this cannot exist. Consequently there is neither love 60 without hope nor hope without love, nor either without faith.

HUMAN SCIENCE IS NOT NECESSARY TO RELIGION

9. When then the question is raised, what is that content III of belief which appertains to religion, there is no call to pry out the secrets of the natural universe as those do whom the Greeks call physicists, nor any need for a Christian to fear to be ignorant of something concerned with the function and 5 number of the elements, the movement and order and phases of the heavenly bodies, the shape of the heavens, the species and natural attributes of animals, fruits, stones, fountains, rivers, and mountains, the measurements of space and time, and the signs of imminent tempests, or of innumerable other 10 facts concerned with those matters which such persons either have discovered or think they have discovered : because not even these have found out everything, though they excel in ability, are aflame with zeal, and abound in leisure, but while they get on the track of some things by human guess-work, 15 and examine others by scientific experiment, yet even in the discoveries they take pride in having made, they are more prolific of opinions than of knowledge. For a Christian it is sufficient to believe that the cause of created things, whether heavenly or earthly, whether visible or invisible, is 20 none other than the goodness of that Creator who is the one

[1] Jas. 2. 19.   [2] Cf. Gal. 5. 6.

true God, and that there is no existent entity which is not
either he or from him ; and that he is a trinity, the Father,
the Son begotten of the Father, and the Holy Spirit proceed-
25 ing from that same Father [and Son], yet one and the same
Spirit of the Father and the Son.

GOD THE CREATOR OF ALL THINGS

10. By this Trinity, which is supremely and equally and
immutably good, all things were created, and while they are
neither supremely nor equally nor immutably good, yet they
are good each in itself; and moreover they are, taken all
5 together, very good, seeing that of them all the marvellous
beauty of the universe consists.

WHY GOD PERMITS EVIL

11. In this universe, even what has the name of evil, when
well ordered and placed in its own position, does the more
notably commend the good things, causing them to be more
pleasing and more laudable by comparison with things evil.
5 For God Almighty (this even the infidels admit—" Power is
his over all things " [1]), being supremely good, would on no
account permit the existence of any admixture of evil in his
works unless he were to such a degree almighty and good as
to bring good even out of evil.   Moreover, that which has
10 the name of evil is nothing else than privation of good.   For
as, in the bodies of animate beings, to be affected by diseases
and wounds is the same thing as to be deprived of health (for
the purpose of healing, when it is applied, is not that those
evils which were in the bodies, namely diseases and wounds,
15 should come out from them and go elsewhere, but that they
should utterly cease to exist: for wound or disease is not a

[1] Virg. *Aen.* 10. 100.

substance in itself, but a defect of fleshly substance, the substance itself being the flesh, evidently a good thing, to which
occur those evils, that is, those deprivations of that goodness
which has the name of health) : so also of minds, whatever 20
defects there are are privations of natural good qualities, and
the healing of these defects is not their transference elsewhere,
but that the defects which did exist in the mind will have no
place to exist, inasmuch as there will be no room for them in
that healthiness.   25

ALL EXISTENCE IS GOOD : EVIL IS A PRIVATION OF GOOD

12. Since therefore the Creator of all natural existences IV
without exception is supremely good, all natural existences are good.   But as, unlike their Creator, they are not
supremely and immutably good, goodness in them is capable
of either decrease or increase.   But for goodness to be de- 5
creased is an evil : albeit, however much it be decreased,
there must needs remain that something (if it is still a natural
existence) by virtue of which it can be a natural existence.
For of what sort soever and however small that natural
existence is, that good which is the natural existence cannot 10
suffer destruction without the destruction of the existence
itself.   A natural existence, when uncorrupted, is rightly
praised : but if it is also incorruptible, so as to be altogether
incapable of being corrupted, it is beyond all doubt much
more worthy of praise.   When, however, it suffers corrup- 15
tion, its corruption is an evil precisely because it deprives it
of some sort of goodness.   For if it deprives it of no goodness,
it does it no harm : but in fact it does do harm : consequently
it takes goodness away from it.   Thus, as long as a natural
existence is suffering corruption, there is present in it good- 20
ness of which it can be deprived : and consequently, if there

remain anything of the natural existence which is now incapable of being corrupted, that natural existence will forthwith be incorruptible : and to this excellent goodness it will attain
25 by process of corruption. If, however, it does not cease to suffer corruption, neither will it altogether cease to possess goodness of which corruption is capable of depriving it. But if corruption succeeds in thoroughly and entirely destroying it, there will remain no goodness in it for precisely
30 the reason that there will remain no natural existence. Consequently, corruption can only destroy goodness by destroying natural existence. It follows then that every natural existence is good—a great good if it cannot suffer corruption, a small good if it can: yet the denial of its goodness is utterly
35 impossible except through folly and ignorance. And if by process of corruption it suffers destruction, not even the corruption itself will survive, seeing there will be no subsistent natural existence for it to exist in.

EVIL CAN ONLY EXIST WHERE THERE IS GOOD

13. Consequently, that which we call evil has no existence except where there is goodness. But goodness devoid of all evil is goodness unalloyed. Goodness, however, in which evil is present is a marred or defective goodness: nor can
5 there ever be any evil where there is no goodness. Hence arises this marvel, that since every natural existence, in so far as it is an existence, is a good thing, the only meaning we can give to the statement that a defective existence is an evil existence is that a thing which is good is evil and that there is
10 no evil thing except such as is good; because every natural existence is a good thing, and no object could be evil, except the object itself which is evil were a natural existence. Thus the only evil that can exist is a goodness of some sort. And although this seems a ridiculous thing to say, yet the sequence

of this reasoning as it were inevitably compels us to say it : 15
and we must take care not to stumble at that prophetic judgement, *Woe unto them that say that good is evil and that evil is
good, who call darkness light and light darkness, who call sweet
bitter and bitter sweet.*[1] Moreover our Lord says, *The evil man
out of the evil treasure of his heart bringeth forth evil things.*[2] Now 20
an evil man must needs be an evil natural existence, seeing
that a man is a natural existence. But if a man, because he is
a natural existence, is a goodness of some sort, what can an
evil man be if not an evil goodness? However, when we
distinguish those two factors, we find his being a man is not 25
the reason for his being an evil, as his being unjust is not the
reason for his being a goodness : but he is a goodness because
he is a man, and an evil because he is unjust. Therefore if
any one says " It is evil to be a man ", or " It is good to be
unjust ", he it is who stumbles at that prophetic judgement, 30
Woe unto them that say that good is evil and that evil is good : for
he is casting aspersions on a work of God, which man is, and
is praising the defect of a man, which injustice is. So then
every natural existence, even if it is a defective one, is good in
so far as it is an existence, and evil in so far as it is defective. 35

THE SAME THING CAN BE AT ONCE GOOD
AND EVIL

14. Consequently in the case of those contradictories which
are known as evil attributes and good, that rule of the logicians
ceases to hold by which they declare that in no object can two
contradictories be present at the same time. For no atmo-
sphere is at the same time dark and light ; no food or drink 5
is at once sweet and bitter ; no body is at the same time black
in the parts where it is white, or at the same time fair in the
places where it is ugly. And this is found to be true in the

[1] Isa. 5. 20.   [2] Matt. 12. 35 ; Luke 6. 45.

case of most and indeed almost all contradictories, that they
10 cannot at the same time coexist in one object. But though
no man questions that good attributes and evil are contradictories, not only can they be present together, but, even
more, evil attributes can only exist at all along with good
things and in good things, though good attributes can exist
15 without evil ones. For a man or an angel can exist and not
be unjust : but an unjust person can only exist if he be a man
or an angel : and he is a good thing because he is a man, a
good thing because he is an angel, and an evil thing because
he is unjust. And these two contradictories to such a degree
20 coexist that if there were no good for it to exist in, the
existence of evil would be utterly impossible : because not
only would it have no ground to stand on, but corruption
would have nothing from which to arise unless there were
something to suffer corruption ; and unless this were some-
25 thing good, it could not suffer corruption, since corruption
is neither more nor less than the extrusion of goodness. From
good things therefore have evil things originated, and only
in good things of some sort do they have their existence.
Nor was there any other source from which a natural exist-
30 ence of evil could have taken its origin. For if there had
been, in so far as it was a natural existence it would necessarily
have been a good one, and either as an incorruptible existence
it would have been a great good, or even as a corruptible
existence it could by no means have existed except as some
35 sort of good, by the corruption of which good the process of
corruption might be capable of doing it injury.

"A GOOD TREE CANNOT BRING FORTH EVIL FRUITS"

15. But when we state that evils have taken their origin
from goods, this should not be supposed to contest our

Lord's judgement in which he affirmed that *A good tree cannot bring forth evil fruits.*[1] For, as the Truth observes, one cannot gather grapes from thorns,[2] for the reason that grapes cannot grow from thorns: yet we do find that from good land both vines and thorns can grow. Similarly, as though it were an evil tree, an evil will cannot bring forth good fruits, that is, good works: yet out of the nature of humanity, which is good, both good will and evil can take their origin. Nor was there any source from which in the first instance the evil will could take its origin, except the nature, which is a good nature, of angel or man. And this the Lord himself most clearly proved, in the same context in which he was speaking of the tree and its fruits: for he observes, *Either make the tree good and its fruit good, or make the tree evil and its fruit evil,*[3] giving fair warning that while it is impossible for evil fruits to come from a good tree, or good fruits from an evil tree, yet it was possible for both sorts of tree to grow out of that soil to which he was speaking.

THE CAUSES OF GOOD AND EVIL

16. This being so, while we approve of that line of Virgil,

> Happy is he
> Who has the skill to search out nature's causes,[4]

we ought not to suppose that it concerns our attainment of felicity that we should know the causes of the great corporal movements in the universe, such as are hid at the most secret bounds of nature,

> Whence the earth doth quake,
> What power doth cause the seas to burst their bars,
> Swelling amain, and on themselves subside,[5]

and the rest of such things. But the causes of good things

---

[1] Matt. 7. 18.   [2] Cf. Matt. 7. 16.   [3] Matt. 12. 33.
[4] Virg. *Georg.* 2. 490.   [5] Ibid. 2. 479.

and evil it is our duty to know, and that to the extent to which it is granted to man, in this life, full of errors and distresses, to know them for the avoidance of these same
15 errors and distresses. In fact we must set our course for that felicity in which we are to be shaken by no distress, misled by no error. For if it were needful for us to know the causes of corporal movements, the causes of our own health would be the first we ought to understand. Yet since, in our ignorance
20 of them, we seek to the physicians, how clear it is with what patience we should bear our ignorance of that which is hidden from us concerning the secrets of heaven and earth.

THE AVOIDANCE OF ERROR

17. For although error ought to be avoided with all the care we can, not only in greater but also in lesser subjects, and although error is impossible except through ignorance of facts, yet it does not follow that one errs just because one is
5 ignorant of something, but because one thinks one knows what one does not know. For in this case one accepts falsehood for truth, which is precisely what error is. Moreover it makes a very great difference in what subject a man goes wrong. For in one and the same subject he who knows is by
10 sound judgement preferred to him who knows not, and he who goes straight to him who goes wrong. But in different subjects, that is, when this man knows these things and that man those, this man more useful things and that man less useful or even harmful, anyone would, in the subjects which
15 the latter knows, count the ignorant superior to him. For there are certain things of which ignorance is better than knowledge. Also it has been known for people to go wrong and profit by it—I mean, in the way of walking, not in the way of character. I myself once happened to make a mistake
20 at a certain cross roads and did not go by the place where an

armed band of Donatists was awaiting my passage: and so
it came about that by an indirect way round I arrived at the
place I was making for, and hearing of those men's ambush
thought myself happy to have gone wrong, and for it gave
thanks to God. Who then would hesitate to count a 25
traveller going wrong like this more happy than the highway-
man who kept the road like that? And it is perhaps for that
reason that in that sublime poet a certain unfortunate lover
speaks and says,

> Thus saw I, thus I met my fate, 30
> Thus evil error seized me,[1]

because there is also a good error which is not only harmless
but even of some benefit. But, on more careful consideration
of the truth, since to err is neither more nor less than to
suppose true what is false or false what is true, or to take the 35
certain for uncertain or the uncertain for certain, whether true
or false, and since this is in the mind a thing just as ugly and
offensive as we feel *Yea, yea; Nay, nay*[2] in narrating or in
assenting to be fine and honest, of a surety even on this
account is this life sorrowful in which we live, that from time 40
to time it has need of error to save it from being lost. God
forbid that that other life should be like this, that life in which
the very Truth is our soul's life, where none deceives, none is
deceived. Here, however, men deceive and are deceived,
and are more to be pitied when by lying they deceive than 45
when by believing liars they are deceived. Yet to such a
degree does a rational nature abhor falsehood, and avoid
error to the fullness of his powers, that even those who love to
deceive are loth to be deceived. For the liar does not regard
himself as erring, but as causing the one who believes him to 50
err: and on that subject indeed which he covers up with his
lie, he is not in error, so long as he knows what the truth is:
but in this he is in error, that he supposes his lie not to be

---

[1] Virg. *Ecl.* 8. 41.   [2] Matt. 5. 37.

harming himself—although every sin causes more harm to
55 him who does it than to him to whom it is done.

VI   18. But here arises a very difficult and dark question,
concerning which, when pressed by the need for an answer,
I have already completed a large book—whether it pertains
to the duty of a righteous man sometimes to tell a lie.   For
5 there are some who go so far as to maintain that at times there
is positive need for a good religious man both to forswear
himself and to utter untruth regarding matters concerned
with divine worship and even regarding the very nature of
God.   But my view is that every lie is a sin, yet that it makes
10 a great difference with what intent and concerning what
subjects each man lies.   For the sin of the man who lies with
the intention of helping another is not as great as his who does
so for hurting: nor does he who by lying directs a traveller
into the wrong road do so much injury as he who by a
15 deceptive lie traduces the way of life.   Of course no man is
to be condemned for lying who speaks a falsehood which he
thinks is true, seeing that as far as concerns himself, he is not
deceiving but is himself deceived.   So then he should not be
accused of lying, though perhaps of overboldness, in that he
20 has without due care given credit to falsehoods and holds
them for true.   And, on the other hand, that man rather is a
liar who utters a truth which he thinks is false; for, as far as
his intention is concerned, inasmuch as he is not expressing
his real thought, he is not speaking truth, even though his
25 statement turn out to be true: nor is any man guiltless of a
lie who with his mouth speaks truth without knowing it,
while in intention he is lying and does know it.   When then
we consider, not the subjects concerning which a statement is

made, but merely the purpose of the speaker, the man who
unwittingly utters a falsehood because he regards it as true 30
is a better man than he who wittingly has the mind to lie,
while ignorant that his statement is true. For the former
does not have one thing in his mind and another in his
words: whereas the latter, whatever the actual quality of
the statement made by him, has yet one thing locked up in 35
his heart and a different one at the end of his tongue: and this
is the specific evil act of a liar. But when we take into
consideration the actual matters spoken of, to this extent it
does matter on what subject a man is mistaken or tells lies,
that though to be mistaken is a lesser evil than to tell a lie, as 40
far as a man's will is concerned, yet it is far more tolerable to
tell a lie in matters unconnected with religion, than to be
mistaken in matters of which the faith and the knowledge are
essential to the service of God. To illustrate this by an
example, let us look how it would be if one person, by a lie, 45
were to report that a certain dead man were alive, while
another person by a mistake were to suppose that after
some long number of years Christ were going to die again:
is not the former manner of lying beyond comparison
preferable to the latter manner of being mistaken? and is it 50
not a matter of much less evil to mislead a person into the
former error than to be misled by someone into the latter?

VARIOUS FORMS AND DEGREES OF ERROR

19. So, then, in some matters our mistakes involve a great
evil, in others a small one, in others none at all, in others even
some sort of good. A man's mistake involves a great evil
when he fails to believe that which leads to life eternal, or
does believe that which leads to eternal death. His mistake 5
involves a small evil when by accepting falsehood for truth
he falls into certain temporal annoyances, which yet the

application of faithful patience converts to good use : as for
example if one, through thinking a bad man to be a good
10 one, were to receive some hurt from him. He, however,
whose belief that a bad man is good, is of such a kind that he
receives no hurt from him, is mistaken at no cost of evil : nor
is he subject to that prophetic rebuke, *Woe to them that call
evil good*.[1] For this must be understood to refer to the vices
15 which make men evil, not to the men themselves. Therefore,
he who says adultery is a good thing is justly judged by that
prophetic word : he, however, who affirms that the man
himself is good, supposing him chaste, and not knowing him
for an adulterer, is mistaken not in the knowledge of things
20 good and evil but in the secrets of human character, when he
calls the man good because he supposes he possesses that
character which he doubts not is good, and affirms that an
adulterer is evil and a chaste man good, yet affirms that this
particular man is good because he does not know he is an
25 adulterer and not chaste. Moreover if a person by going astray
escapes destruction, as I remarked above once happened to
me on a journey, even some degree of good accrues to the
man by his straying. But when I allege that in some matters
a person's mistakenness involves no evil but even some sort
30 of good, it is not the straying itself that I allege to be no evil
or even some sort of good, but the evil one avoids by straying
or the good one arrives at by it : the question being what it is
that because of the straying fails to occur, or that does result. For
the straying itself and of itself is in a great matter a great evil, in
35 a small matter a small one, but always an evil. For who except
a man astray will deny that it is an evil to accept falsehoods for
truths, or to reject truths as falsehoods, or to regard uncertain
things as certain or certain things as uncertain? But it is one
thing to suppose a man good when he is bad—which is
40 an error : and it is quite another thing to escape another evil

[1] Isa. 5. 20.

as the consequence of this one, in the case when no harm is
done by the bad man who was supposed good.   Also it is
one thing to suppose that that is the right road which is not
the right road, and quite another thing in consequence of this
mistake to obtain some sort of benefit, as, for example, 45
deliverance from the schemes of evil men.

NOT EVERY MISTAKE IS A SIN

20. Indeed I am in some doubt whether we should even VII
give the name of sins to errors such as these—as when a person
has a good opinion of a bad man, being ignorant of his real
character : or when, instead of the things we perceive by our
bodily senses, there occur similar things which are perceived by 5
the spirit as though by the body, or by the body as though
by the spirit (as the apostle Peter supposed to be the case when
he thought he saw a vision when unexpectedly released from
prison and fetters by an angel [1]) : or when in corporal things
themselves a thing is supposed to be smooth when it is rough 10
or sweet when it is bitter or to smell pleasantly when it stinks,
or one thinks it thunders when a wagon passes, or that it is
such and such a person when it is someone else, when there
are two very like one another as often happens in the case of
twins (of which the poet observes " an error grateful to their 15
sire " [2]), and other things of this sort.   Nor have I at this
juncture undertaken the solution of that very involved
question which has tormented the perspicacious Academics,
whether the philosopher ought ever to assent to anything,
for fear of falling into error if he assents to falsehoods as 20
though true, seeing that, as they allege, all things are either
hidden or uncertain.   On this I wrote three books at the
beginning of my conversion, so that objections met with on
the threshold might not be a hindrance to me.   And in fact

[1] Acts 12. 9.   [2] Virg. Aen. 10. 392.

25 it was necessary to clear away despair of discovering the truth, a despair which does have the appearance of being strengthened by those men's arguments. With them therefore every mistake is supposed to be a sin, and they claim that such sin cannot be avoided, unless all assent be withheld. In
30 fact they allege that anyone is in error who assents to things uncertain; and in incisive but overweening disputations they maintain that there is nothing certain in human perceptions, in view of the undistinguishable similarity of what is false, even if the thing perceived chance to be true. But among us
35 *the just man lives by faith.*[1] Yet if assent be withheld, faith also is withheld, because without assent there is no believing. And there are things true, though they be not seen, belief in which is a condition prerequisite to the attainment of the happy life, which can only mean eternal life. Whether,
40 however, we ought to discourse with these men, I know not: for they are ignorant not only that they will live for ever but even that they are living now—or rather they profess to be ignorant, though of a fact it is impossible for them to be ignorant of. For it is not permissible for anyone to
45 be ignorant that he is alive, seeing that if he is not alive he cannot even be ignorant of anything: for not only knowledge, but even ignorance, is an attribute of one who is alive. But, it appears, by refusing to admit that they are alive, they think they are taking precaution against error, though even
50 by being in error they are proved to be alive: for a man who is not alive cannot be in error. As, then, not only is it true, but we know it to be true, that we are alive, so there are also many things true, and known to be true, to which the refusal of assent, so far from being good philosophy, is sheer madness,
55 and should be so called.

[1] Hab. 2. 4; Rom. 1. 17; Heb. 10. 38.

BUT ALL MISTAKES ARE EVIL

21. But with regard to matters in which it makes no difference to one's attaining to the kingdom of God whether they are believed or not, or whether they are, or are supposed to be, either true or false, to go astray in these, that is, to substitute one supposition for another, should not be regarded 5 as a sin—or, if it is, a very small and trivial one.   Lastly, whatever its nature and its magnitude, it has no concern with that road by which we are making our way to God: for this road is the faith of Christ, which worketh by affection.[1]   From this road that " error grateful to their sire " in the case of 10 the twin boys constituted no divergence: nor did the apostle Peter diverge from this road when, thinking he saw a vision, he substituted one supposition for another to the extent that he only distinguished the veritable bodies among which he was, from the ghosts of bodies among which he thought 15 himself to be, when the angel by whose agency he was set free had departed from him.   Nor did the patriarch Jacob diverge from this road when, though his son was alive, he believed some evil beast had slain him.   For in these and similar falsehoods we suffer deception without prejudice to the faith we 20 have towards God, and stray without deserting the road which leads us to him.   Yet even if these mistakes are not sins, yet are they to be reckoned among the evils of this life, which is to this extent subject to vanity, that here we accept false things for true, reject true things as false, and cling to uncertain things 25 as if certain.   For though these have no part in that faith, that true and certain faith, by which we are moving towards eternal blessedness, yet they are a part of that misery in which we yet remain.   Truly by no means should we be subject to deception by any sensation of either mind or body, if we 30 were already in enjoyment of that true and perfect felicity.

[1] Gal. 5. 6.

D

THE LESS SERIOUS KIND OF LIE

22. For all that, every lie must for this reason be described as sin, because man's duty is—not only when he knows for himself what is true but even when, as a man, he is astray and deceived—to speak that which he has in his mind, whether
5 that be true or be supposed true when it is not: whereas every man who utters a lie is, by his will to deceive, speaking the opposite of what he thinks in his mind. And yet the purpose for which words were appointed was not that by them men should deceive one another but that by them one man should
10 bring his thoughts to another man's cognizance. Thus, to use words for deception, and not for their intended purpose, is a sin. And the fact that we can sometimes confer benefits by lying, is no reason for supposing that there is any lie which is not a sin. For we can at times confer benefits by thieving,
15 if the poor man to whom the gift is openly given perceives the advantage, while the rich man from whom it is stealthily taken perceives no disadvantage: yet no one would affirm that such a theft is not a sin. We can do so also by committing adultery, if it appears that some woman will die of
20 love unless her wishes are met in this respect, while if she remains alive she will be cleansed by penitence; yet not for that reason will one deny that such adultery is a sin. But if we approve of chastity—as we rightly do—what offence has truth committed, that for another person's utility the one
25 may not be debauched by adultery, while the other may be by lying? [It is not possible for a lie to be sometimes counted praiseworthy, on the ground that we occasionally tell lies to ensure people's benefit. So then, a lie is a sin, though a venial one; good intention may be its excuse, though falsity
30 is its condemnation.] That men have advanced to very great honour who tell lies solely to ensure a man's safety, does not admit of denial: but in this advancement of theirs the well-

deserved praise, or even the temporal reward, is given to
their benevolence, not to their deceit: the latter may perhaps
be forgiven, but should not be the subject of encomiums, 35
especially among the heirs of the New Covenant, who are
told, *Let your speech be, Yea, yea; Nay, nay: for what is more
is of the evil*.[1]   And on account of this evil, because in this
mortal life it ceases not to creep in, even the fellow-heirs of
Christ repeat, *Forgive us our debts*.[2]   40

SUMMARY: THE CAUSES OF GOOD AND EVIL

23. We have discussed these matters, with the brevity VIII
required by the present work, because we have to know the
causes of things good and evil, at least in so far as suffices for
the way which should lead us to that kingdom in which there
will be life without death, truth without error, felicity with- 5
out discomposure: and we ought never to doubt that of the
good things which are our lot the sole and only cause is the
goodness of God, while of the evil things the cause is that the
will of that mutable good, the angel first, the man afterwards, falls short of that good which is immutable.   10

DERIVATIVE EVILS, IGNORANCE AND
CONCUPISCENCE

24. This is the first of the rational creature's evils, that is,
his first privation of good.   After that, even against men's
will, has crept in ignorance of the things that ought to be
done, along with concupiscence of things hurtful, in whose
train follow their attendants, error and sorrow: and when 5
these two evils are perceived to be impending, the emotion
of the mind as it shrinks from them is called fear.   Moreover, when the mind obtains the things desired, deadly or

---

[1] Matt. 5. 37.   [2] Matt. 6. 12.

useless as they are, seeing that by its error it fails to perceive
10 this, it is overcome by unwholesome delight or even puffed
up with empty joy. From these springs of unwholesome-
ness, springs not of bounty but of indigence, flows every
misery of our rational nature.

THE PENALTY OF DEATH

25. Yet, in the midst of its own evils, this rational nature
has not contrived to lose its appetite for blessedness. Rather,
these are evils common to men and to angels, condemned
for their own malice by the righteousness of the Lord. But
5 man has also his peculiar penalty, being punished by the death
of his body besides. God had in fact threatened him with
the punishment of death if he were to sin: [1] for he gave him
the gift of free choice, and yet, so as to keep him under control
by his commandment, put him in fear of destruction. So he
10 placed him in the felicity of paradise, as it were in a mirrored
image of life, so that from there he might by observing
righteousness climb up to better things.

ORIGINAL SIN

26. Made an exile from thence after his sin, he bound also
his offspring, whom by sinning he had marred in himself as
root, in the penalty of death and damnation: with the result
that all the children born of him and of the wife condemned
5 with him (her through whom he had sinned), being born of
the carnal concupiscence which was imposed as a penalty
akin to their disobedience, were infected with original sin,
and by it were to be dragged through divers errors and
sorrows towards that final and endless torment along with
10 the revolted angels, their spoilers and impropriators and

[1] Gen. 2. 17.

copartners. Thus *by one man sin entered into the world, and death by means of sin: and so it passed over into all men, in that all sinned.*[1] By "world" in this text the apostle meant, of course, the entire human race.

GOD'S RIGHTEOUSNESS, AND HIS MERCY

27. This then was the situation. The whole lump of the human race, being under condemnation, was lying down in evils, nay rather was wallowing in them, and was being hurled headlong into ever deeper evils, and, being attached to the faction of those angels who had sinned, was paying 5 the well-deserved penalty of its impious revolt. Indeed the righteous wrath of God is closely concerned with whatever it is that by blind and uncontrolled concupiscence evil men do wilfully, and with whatever by manifest and apparent penalties they suffer unwillingly : not indeed that the Creator's 10 goodness ceases either to continue to supply life and quickening potency to evil angels (for if the continuance of this supply be withheld, life ceases) or, in the case of men who come to birth, though of a marred and condemned stock, to give form and life to the seed, to order their members 15 through periods of time, to quicken their perceptions through extensions of space, and to grant them sustenance. For he judged it better to bring good out of evil than to preclude evil from existing. And if indeed it had been his will that there should be no possible reformation of men for the better, 20 as there is none in the case of the impious angels, would it not deservedly have come about that the natural creature which has revolted against God and by the evil use of its own capacities has trodden under foot and transgressed the commandment of its own Creator (which it would have 25 been quite easy for it to keep), which by obstinately turning

[1] Rom. 5. 12.

its back on its Creator's light has done violence to his image
in itself, and by an evil use of free choice has broken loose
from his laws and his salutary servitude—that this natural
30 creature should in its entirety be for ever abandoned by him
and should in accordance with its own deserts pay an everlasting penalty?   Clearly so God would act, were he merely
righteous and not also merciful, displaying his own unmerited mercy much more evidently by the deliverance even
35 of those who do not deserve it.

THE FALL OF THE REVOLTED ANGELS: THE EVERLASTING FELICITY OF THE OTHERS

IX   28. While then some of the angels, being through impious
pride in revolt from God, have been cast down from their
lofty heavenly habitation into the lower darkness of this air,
the residue of the angels has remained with God in eternal
5 beatitude and sanctity.   For these others were not engendered
of one angel who fell and was condemned: in that case, as
with men, the primal evil would have held them bound in
the chains of a guilty succession and would be dragging all
without exception to merited penalties: but rather when
10 that one who has become the devil was elated along with his
companions in impiety, and was cast down with them
through this very elation, the rest in pious obedience adhered
to their Lord, and received, what those others had not, such
firm knowledge as would give them assurance of their own
15 everlasting and for ever unshakable stability.

GOD'S PURPOSE FOR MANKIND

29. It was then the good pleasure of God, the Creator and
Governor of the universe, that as it was not the whole multi-
tude of the angels which had perished by revolting from
God, those who had perished should abide in continual

perdition, while those who on the revolt of these had 5
remained steadfast with God should rejoice in the assured
knowledge of their own ever-continuing felicity: but that,
since the rest of rational creation, which consisted in mankind, had all of it perished by sins and punishments both
original and each man's own, out of part of it restored 10
should be filled up the gap in the angelic company caused by
that diabolic collapse. For this is the promise made to the
saints as they rise again, that they will be equal with the
angels of God.[1] Thus will that Jerusalem on high, our
mother the city of God, be deprived of none of its full 15
complement of citizens, or even perhaps will reign in more
fertile abundance. For we know neither the numbers of
the holy men, nor those of the foul demons into whose place
will succeed these sons of our holy mother [the Church],
who used to appear sterile on earth:[2] but these will abide 20
without any bound of time in that peace from which those
fell away. But the numbers of those citizens, both the
number which is and that which is to be, are in the full view
of that Artificer who calleth the things that are not, even as
the things that are,[3] and hath disposed all things in measure 25
and number and weight.[4]

NEITHER BY MERIT NOR BY FREE CHOICE, BUT BY THE GRACE OF GOD

30. But can this part of the human race to which God has
promised deliverance and an eternal kingdom—can it obtain
restoration by the merits of its own works? God forbid!
For what good work can one that is lost accomplish, except
in so far as he has been freed from perdition? Can he do 5
anything by the free exercise of his choice? Again, God

[1] Cf. Matt. 22. 30.   [2] Cf. Isa. 54. 1; Gal. 4. 27.
[3] Rom. 4. 17.   [4] Wisd. 11. 20.

forbid! For by the evil use of free choice man has destroyed
both himself and it. For as one who kills himself, certainly
by being alive kills himself, but by killing himself ceases to
10 live, and can have no power to restore himself to life after
the killing; so, when sin was committed by free choice, sin
became victor and free choice was lost. *For of whom a man
is overcome, to the same is he also brought in bondage as a servant.*[1]
Assuredly this is the apostle Peter's judgement. And seeing
15 it is a true one, what liberty, I ask you, can a servant in
bondage have, except when it delights him to sin? For
only he is free in service who gladly does the will of his Lord.
And consequently he who is the servant of sin is free only
for sinning. Wherefore he cannot be free to act righteously
20 unless he is made free from sin and has begun to be a servant
of righteousness. This is the true liberty, because of joy for
the upright act; and no less is it pious servitude, because of
obedience to the commandment. But whence shall a man
declared a bondman, and sold, obtain that liberty for well-
25 doing, except he be redeemed by him who says, *If the Son
shall make you free, then shall ye be free indeed*? [2] But until
this begins to take place in a man, how shall one who is not
yet free for well-doing, boast himself concerning free choice
in a good work, unless he be lifting up himself, puffed up
30 with the vain pride which the apostle restrains with the
words, *By grace are ye saved, through faith*? [3]

FAITH IS ITSELF A GIFT OF GOD

31. And lest men should claim that faith at any rate was
their own, and thus fail to understand that it is theirs by
divine granting, as the apostle says elsewhere that he had
obtained mercy to be faithful,[4] so here also he has added,

---

[1] 2 Pet. 2. 19.   [2] John 8. 36.
[3] Eph. 2. 8.   [4] Cf. 1 Cor. 7. 25.

And this not of ourselves, but it is a gift of God, not as a result of 5
works, lest perchance one should be exalted.[1]   And lest it should
be supposed that the faithful would be lacking in good
works, again he added, *For we are his formation, created in
Christ Jesus in good works, which God hath prepared beforehand
that we should walk in them.*[2]   Then therefore are we truly 10
made to be free when God shapes, that is, forms and creates
us,[3] so that we may be not merely men (he has made us that
already) but good men: and this he is now doing by his
grace, so that in Christ Jesus we may be a new creature,
according to the saying, *Create in me a clean heart, O God.*[4] 15
For, as concerns the nature of the human heart, God had
already created his heart [: but what the prophet is asking for
is a renewal of the soul which dwells in the heart].

BOTH TO WILL AND TO WORK IS OF GOD

32. Also, lest any man should glory, not indeed of the
works, but of the free choice of his will, as though from
himself originated the merit to which, like the paying of a
debt, liberty itself were returned as the reward of well-doing,
let him hear the same herald of grace when he says, *For it is* 5
*God that worketh in us both to will and to work according to good
will:* [5] and, in another place, *So it is not of him that willeth,
nor of him that runneth, but of God that hath mercy.*[6]   Since
there is no doubt that, if a man is of such an age as to have
the use of reason, he can neither believe, hope, nor love, 10
unless by an act of will, nor attain to the prize of the high
calling of God unless he has run willingly, how then is it not
of him that willeth nor of him that runneth but of God that
hath mercy, except that the will itself, as it is written, is
prepared beforehand by God? [7]   Otherwise, if the meaning 15

---

[1] Eph. 2. 8, 9.   [2] Eph. 2. 10.   [3] Cf. Gen. 2. 7.
[4] Ps. 51. 10.   [5] Phil. 2. 13.   [6] Rom. 9. 16.   [7] LXX Prov. 8. 35.

of the expression, *Not of him that willeth, nor of him that runneth,
but of God that hath mercy*, is that it is the result of both things,
the will of man and the mercy of God, so that we should
understand the expression *Not of him that willeth, nor of him
20 that runneth, but of God that hath mercy* as though the meaning
were, " The will of man alone is not sufficient unless there be
also the mercy of God ", in that case even the mercy of God
is not sufficient by itself, unless there be also the will of man :
and consequently, if the expression is right, *It is not of* the
25 man *that willeth, but of God that hath mercy*, because the will of
a man by itself does not accomplish it, why should not also
the contrary expression be right, " It is not of God that hath
mercy, but of the man that willeth ", on the ground that the
mercy of God by itself does not accomplish it?   In short,
30 if no Christian will dare to say " It is not of God that hath
mercy, but of the man that willeth ", lest he openly contra-
dict the apostle, it remains for us to understand that the
expression, *It is not of him that willeth, nor of him that runneth,
but of God that hath mercy*, is correct in that the whole is
35 assigned to God, who both prepares beforehand man's good
will to be assisted, and assists it when prepared.   For a man's
good will does precede many gifts of God, though not all :
but itself is among those which it does not itself precede.
For both these are read in the sacred oracles, both *His mercy
40 shall anticipate me* [1] and *His mercy shall follow me*.[2]   Him that
will not, it anticipates, so that it may become his will : him
that will, it follows, that his willing may not be in vain.   For
why are we admonished to pray for our enemies, evidently
those who are unwilling to live a godly life, except that God
45 may work in them also the will?   Also why are we admonished to ask so that we may receive, except that what we
wish for may be brought to pass by him who has brought it
to pass that we wish for it?   We pray then for our enemies,

---

[1] LXX Ps. 58. 11 (59. 10).   [2] Ps. 23. 6.

that the mercy of God may anticipate them, as it has also
anticipated us: we pray also for ourselves, that his mercy 50
may follow us.

"CHILDREN OF WRATH" IN NEED OF A MEDIATOR

33. Thus the human race was held in righteous condemna- X
tion, and they were all children of wrath. Of this wrath it
is written: *For all our days are consumed away, and in thy
wrath have we ceased to be: our years will make designs as doth
a spider.*[1] Of this wrath Job also observes: *Man that is born of* 5
a woman is short of life and full of wrath.[2] Of this wrath also
the Lord Jesus observes: *He that believeth in the Son hath
eternal life: but he that believeth not in the Son hath not life, but
the wrath of God abideth upon him.*[3] He says not " will come "
but " abideth upon him ". In fact this wrath accompanies 10
every man's birth: which is why the apostle observes, *For
we also were by nature children of wrath, even as the others.*[4]
Since men were in this wrath through original sin, and that
the more seriously and destructively the more they added
greater and more frequent sins, there was need for a mediator, 15
that is, a reconciler, who should propitiate this wrath by the
offering of that one and only sacrifice of which all the
sacrifices of the Law and the Prophets were shadows cast
beforehand. Of this the apostle observes: *For if, when we
were enemies, we were reconciled to God by the death of his Son,* 20
*much more, being reconciled now in his blood, we shall be safe from
the wrath through him.*[5] But when they speak of God " being
wroth ", they are not suggesting any agitation of his, such as
is in the mind of a man who is wroth; but, by the borrowing
of the term from human emotions, his vengeance, which 25
cannot but be righteous, has had the name " wrath " given

[1] LXX Ps. 89. 9 (90. 9).   [2] Job 14. 1.   [3] John 3. 36.
[4] Eph. 2. 3.   [5] Rom. 5. 10, 9.

to it. The fact then that we by a Mediator are being
reconciled to God, and do receive the Holy Spirit, so as,
instead of enemies, to be made into sons—*for as many as are*
30 *being led by the Spirit of God, these are sons of God*[1]—this is
the grace of God through Jesus Christ our Lord.

THE VIRGINAL CONCEPTION AND NATIVITY
OF CHRIST

34. Of this Mediator it would take too long to say all the
things it were meet to say—indeed, no man could say them
as is meet. For who can explain in appropriate language
this single fact, that *the Word was made flesh and dwelt among*
5 *us*,[2] so that our faith might be in the only Son of God the
Father Almighty, born of the Holy Spirit and Mary the
Virgin? This at least we say: that the Word was made flesh
through the assuming of flesh by divinity, not by the
conversion of divinity into flesh. By "flesh" here we must
10 understand "manhood", the expression indicating the whole
by its part, as in the text, *Because by the works of the law shall
no flesh be justified*,[3] meaning "no man". For it is intolerable
to say that in that assumption of human nature any part of it
was lacking. Yet was that nature in every sense free from
15 every bond of sin: not as one is when born of both sexes
through carnal concupiscence with trespass as entail, the
guilt of which is washed away by regeneration; but as one
must needs be who was born of a virgin, conceived by his
mother's faith, not by passion. Yea even if at his nativity
20 her virginity were to be broken, in such a case he would not
be born of a virgin, and (which God forbid!) the whole
Church would be making a false profession that he was born
of the Virgin Mary—though daily does this Church, in
imitation of his mother, give birth to his members, while

[1] Rom. 8. 14.   [2] John 1. 14.   [3] Rom. 3. 20.

remaining a virgin.   Read, if you will, my letter concerning 25
the Virginity of Saint Mary, which I wrote to the right
honourable Volusianus, whose name I mention with respect
and affection.

SON OF GOD AND SON OF MAN

35. Consequently Christ Jesus, the Son of God, is both
God and Man: God before all ages, man in our age: God
because he is God's Word (for *the Word was God*[1]), man
however because into unity of person with the Word has
been joined a rational soul, and flesh.   Therefore, in that he 5
is God, he and the Father are one,[2] while in that he is man,
the Father is greater than he.[3]   For, being the only Son of
God, by nature and not by grace, that he might even be full
of grace he was made also Son of Man: and he, being one,
is both things, one Christ constituted of both: because, being 10
in the form of God, he regarded not as robbery that which
he was by nature, that is, equal with God.   Yet he emptied
himself, taking the form of a servant, without either losing or
diminishing the form of God.[4]   And consequently he both
was made less and remained equal, and, being himself one, 15
was both of these, as I have said: yet one of them for the
Word's sake, the other for the sake of the manhood: for
the Word's sake equal with the Father, for the manhood's
sake less: one Son of God, the same also Son of Man: one
Son of Man, the same also Son of God: not two sons of 20
God, God and a man, but one Son of God: God without
beginning, Man since a definite beginning: our Lord Jesus
Christ.

[1] John 1. 1.   [2] John 10. 30.
[3] John 14. 28.   [4] Cf. Phil. 2. 6, 7.

THE INCARNATION A NOTABLE EVIDENCE OF THE
GRACE OF GOD

XI   36. Here surely is an altogether noble and manifest commendation of the grace of God. What deserts had human
nature acquired in Christ as man, that it should on this sole
occasion have been assumed into the unity of the Person of
5 the only Son of God?   What good will, the pursuit of what
good purpose, what good works, had preceded by which
such a man should make himself worthy to be made one
person with God? Is it that there had previously been a
man, and that there was granted him this singular benefit
10 for having singularly deserved well of God? No: from
the time that that Man's existence began, that Man began
to be none other than the Son of God, the only Son: and
for God the Word's sake, who by assuming that manhood
was made flesh, he was necessarily God, that as each and
15 every man is one person, being rational soul, and flesh, so
Christ should be one person, the Word and Man. Whence
should human nature have such great glory, a glory un-
doubtedly freely granted for no precedent deserts, except
that here is evidently displayed, if one but faithfully and
20 modestly consider it, the greatness of God's grace, and that
alone?—that men may understand that they are being
justified from sins by that same grace by which it came to
pass that Christ as Man was incapable of any sin. In these
terms also the angel saluted his mother when announcing to
25 her this birth that was to be: *Hail, thou that art full of grace*:
and shortly afterwards, *Thou hast found grace with God.*[1]
She indeed is addressed as full of grace, and as having found
grace with God, that she might be the mother of her Lord,
yea more, the Lord of all: but of Christ himself John the
30 Evangelist, having said *And the Word was made flesh and dwelt*

---

[1] Luke I. 28, 30.

among us, added, *And we have seen his glory, the glory as of the only-begotten of the Father, and he was full of grace and truth.*[1] "The Word was made flesh" is equivalent to "he was full of grace": "the glory of the only-begotten of the Father" means "full of truth". For that Truth itself, by nature 35 and not by grace the only-begotten Son of God, did by grace assume manhood in such close unity of person, as himself and of himself to be also the Son of Man.

"THE HOLY GHOST SHALL COME UPON THEE"

37. For this same Jesus Christ, the only-begotten (that is, the one and only) Son of God, our Lord, was born of the Holy Spirit and Mary the Virgin. Now of course the Holy Spirit is the gift of God—though this gift is equal with its Giver, and therefore the Holy Spirit also is God, no less great 5 than the Father and the Son. The fact then that according to his manhood Christ's birth is of the Holy Spirit, is neither more nor less than a demonstration of grace itself. For when the Virgin asked the angel how this that he was announcing to her should be, seeing she knew not a man, the angel 10 answered, *The Holy Ghost shall come upon thee, and the power of the Most High shall overshadow thee: therefore also that holy thing that shall be born of thee shall be called the Son of God.*[2] And when Joseph was minded to put her away, suspecting adultery since he knew he was not the child's father, he 15 received a similar answer from the angel: *Fear not to take unto thee Mary thy wife, for that which is born in her is of the Holy Ghost*—that is, what you suspect is due to another man, is due to the Holy Ghost.[3]

[1] John I. 14.   [2] Luke I. 34, 35.   [3] Matt. I. 19, 20.

MARY IS CHRIST'S MOTHER : THE HOLY GHOST
IS NOT HIS FATHER

XII   38. Are we then to say that the Holy Spirit is the father of
Christ as man, as if God the Father begat the Word, and the
Holy Spirit begat the manhood, so that of these two
substances should consist one Christ, who should be both the
5 Father's son as concerning the Word and the Holy Spirit's
son as concerning the manhood, as though the Holy Spirit,
as if he were his father, had begotten him of a virgin mother?
None will be bold enough to suggest this : nor is there need
to prove by argument how many outrageous consequences
10 would follow, since the suggestion itself is so outrageous as
to be intolerable to Christian ears.   Certainly, as our Creed
has it : " Our Lord Jesus Christ, who is God from God, and
yet as man was born of the Holy Spirit and Mary the Virgin,
is in both substances, the divine and the human, the one and
15 only Son of God the Father Almighty, from whom
proceedeth the Holy Spirit."   In what sense then do we
mean that Christ was born of the Holy Spirit, if the Holy
Spirit was not his begetter?   Is it that he made him?   For
in that our Lord Jesus Christ is God, *All things were made by
20 him* : [1] but in that he is man, he himself also was made, as
the apostle says, *He was made of the seed of David according to
the flesh*.[2]   But that created thing which the Virgin conceived
and bore, though it appertains to the person of the Son alone,
yet was made by the whole Trinity—for the works of the
25 Trinity cannot be assigned to the Persons separably.   Why
then, in the making of it, is only the Holy Spirit mentioned?
Is it that when the name of one of the Three is mentioned
in connexion with any operation, the whole Trinity is understood to be operating?   That in fact is the case, as can be
30 shown by many instances : though we must not delay over

---

[1] John 1. 3.   [2] Rom. 1. 3.

this any longer.   What now concerns us is the meaning of
the expression " born of the Holy Spirit " when he is in no
sense the son of the Holy Spirit.   Now this world of ours
was made by God : yet we may not on that account say it
is God's son, or that it was born of God, but that it was made 35
or created or founded or established, or whatever expression
of the kind we may rightly use.   In the present case therefore,
when we state our faith that he was born of the Holy Spirit
and Mary the Virgin, it is not easy to explain in what manner
he is not the son of the Holy Spirit but is the son of the 40
Virgin Mary, though his birth is due to both : yet is there no
room for doubt that he was not born of the Spirit as father,
while he was born of the Virgin as mother.

SOME FORMS OF BIRTH DO NOT CONSTITUTE SONSHIP

39. So then we cannot admit that everything that is born
of something else must inevitably be designated the son of
that something.   I need not mention that in the case of man,
the birth of a son is of one sort, of quite another that of a
hair, a louse, or a tapeworm, none of which is a son.   But, 5
to leave these out as being too inelegant for comparison with
so great a subject, it remains true that those who are born of
water and the Holy Spirit [1] could never be rightly said to be
sons of the water, for evidently they are described as the sons
of God as father and of the Church as mother.   In this 10
manner therefore was born of the Holy Spirit he who is the
Son of God the Father, but not the son of the Holy Spirit.
For the mention we made of hair and the rest has at least the
value of reminding us that not everything that is born of
something else can also be described as the son of that of 15
which it is born : as likewise it does not follow that all who

[1] Cf. John 3. 5.

E

are described as a particular man's sons need also be described
as having been born of him—as is the case with those who
are adopted. Also those described as sons of hell [1] are not
20 those born of hell but those prepared beforehand for it, just
as the sons of the kingdom [2] are being prepared beforehand
for the kingdom.

THE HOLY SPIRIT IS GOD'S GRACIOUS GIFT

40. Since then one thing can be born of another in such a
fashion as not to be its son, and conversely not everyone
described as a son has been born of him whose son he is
called, doubtless that fashion in which Christ was born of
5 the Holy Spirit not as son, but of Mary the Virgin as son,
suggests to us the grace of God by which Man, not for any
precedent deserts, was at the very outset and first beginning
of his natural existence linked with God the Word into such
unity of person that the same one who was the Son of Man
10 should also be the Son of God, and the same who was the
Son of God should be the Son of Man, and that thus in his
assumption of human nature grace itself should be in some
manner a natural attribute of that Man—grace such as to
exclude all possibility of sin. And this grace must needs
15 have been indicated by the mention of the Holy Spirit, seeing
that he himself in his own being is God in such manner as
also to be described as God's gift. But to discourse adequately
of this matter, if indeed such a thing were possible, would
require a greatly extended discussion.

CHRIST, WITHOUT SIN, WAS MADE SIN FOR US

XIII   41. So then he was engendered, or rather conceived,
apart from any pleasure of carnal concupiscence, and thus

[1] Cf. Matt. 23. 15.   [2] Cf. Matt. 13. 38.

had contracted no sin by reason of his origin : moreover by
the grace of God he was in a marvellous and ineffable manner
conjoined and interknit in unity of person with the Father's 5
only-begotten Word, who is not by grace but by nature the
Son, and therefore himself committed no sin : yet because
of the likeness of sinful flesh in which he came, he was himself described as sin,[1] seeing he was to be sacrificed for the
washing away of sins. In fact in the old law sacrifices for 10
sins were called by the name of " sins " :[2] and he became
that in truth of which those sacrifices were shadows. Hence
the apostle, having said, *We beseech you for Christ's sake, to be
reconciled to God*, immediately added the remark, *Him that
knew no sin he hath made to be sin instead of us, so that we may be* 15
the righteousness of God in him.[3] He did not say, as we read
it in certain faulty copies, " He who knew no sin hath made
sin instead of us ", as though instead of us Christ himself had
sinned : he says rather, *Him that knew no sin* (meaning Christ)
God to whom we need to be reconciled *hath made to be sin* 20
instead of us, meaning a sacrifice for sins through which we
might have power to be reconciled. He himself then is
the " sin ", *so that we may be the righteousness*, not our own
but *of God*, not in ourselves but *in him* : even as he himself
made a show of the sin,[4] not his but ours, nor having its basis 25
in him but in us, by the likeness of the sinful flesh [5] in which
he was crucified, to the extent that since in him was no sin he
might in some sort die to sin [6] while dying to the flesh in
which was the likeness of sin, yet, since he himself had never
lived according to the ancientry of sin, he might by his 30
resurrection place the seal on our new life which was being
quickened again from the ancient death whereby we had
been dead in sin.[7]

BAPTISM, A DEATH UNTO SIN:

42. This and none other is that great mystery of baptism which is celebrated in us, that all those who appertain to that grace should die to sin (just as he is described as having died to sin because he died to the flesh, the likeness of sin) and 5 should live by being born again from the font (as he did by rising again from the tomb), whatever the age of their body may be.[1]

IN BOTH YOUNG AND OLD

43. For, from the babe newly born right on to the tottering elder, as none may be kept back from baptism, so there is none who does not die to sin in baptism. But babes die only to original sin, the elder however to all those further sins which 5 by evil living they have added to that which they contracted by being born.

SIN, SINGULAR AND PLURAL

44. Now the common expression implies that it is sin itself they die to, though it is perfectly clear that they die not to one sin but to many, indeed to all the sins they have committed in their own person, whether by thought or word 5 or deed: the reason being that the plural is frequently indicated by the singular, as the poet says,

Its womb with armoured warrior do they fill,[2]

though they filled it with a number of warriors. Also in our own Writings we read, *Pray thou therefore unto the Lord,* 10 *that he take away the serpent from us*:[3] it does not say "serpents", though it was serpents the people were suffering from, that made them say this. And there are numberless

---

[1] Cf. Rom. 6. 2 ff.   [2] Virg. *Aen.* 2. 20.   [3] Num. 21. 7.

such instances. When, however, that singular original sin
is indicated by the plural, when we say that infants are
baptized " for the remission of sins " (not " for the remission 15
of the sin "), this is the contrary form of expression by which
the singular is indicated by the plural. For example, in the
Gospel, when Herod was dead, the statement was made,
They are dead that sought the boy's life,[1] not " he is dead " : and
in Exodus, *They made for themselves gods of gold*,[2] when it was 20
only one calf they made; and of it they said, *These be thy
gods, O Israel, which have brought thee out from the land of
Egypt*,[3] here too putting the plural for the singular.

MANY SINS IN ONE

45. And yet even in that single sin which by one man
entered into the world, which also has passed over into all
men,[4] that sin on account of which even infants are baptized,
can be distinguished a number of sins, if that one be as it were
divided into its several members. For there is pride there, 5
in that man delighted rather to be under his own authority
than under God's. There is sacrilege, in that he disbelieved
God. There is murder, in that he hurled himself down to
death. There is spiritual fornication, in that the virginity
of the human mind was debauched by the serpent's solicita- 10
tion. There is theft, in that there was unlawful seizure of
forbidden food. There is avarice, in that he contrived to get
more than he ought to have needed—and all the rest that by
careful reckoning can be discovered in this single unlawful
act.   15

[1] Matt. 2. 20.   [2] Ex. 32. 31.
[3] Ex. 32. 4.   [4] Cf. Rom. 5. 12.

"THE SINS OF THE FATHERS"

46. Also it is alleged, and not without good reason, that infants are involved in their parents' sins—not those only of the first man and woman, but those of their own parents of whom they were actually born. Certainly that divine
5 sentence, *I will visit the sins of the fathers upon the children,*[1] binds them, at least until by means of regeneration they begin to belong to the New Testament. This testament became the subject of prophecy when the statement was made through Ezekiel that sons would not inherit the sins of their fathers,
10 and that there should no longer be this proverb in Israel, *The fathers have eaten the sour grapes and the children's teeth have had a shock.*[2] For the purpose of each person's rebirth is that there should be paid up in him the whole amount of the sin born along with him. For sins which by ill-doing are
15 committed afterwards can be healed also by penitence, as we see happening even after baptism. Thus the only reason for the establishment of regeneration was that generation itself is at fault—so much so that even one begotten of lawful matrimony says, *I was conceived in iniquities, and in sins did my*
20 *mother nourish me in the womb.*[3] He too says, not "in iniquity" or "in sin", though this too would be a correct expression: but he preferred to say "iniquities" and "sins", because even in that one sin, which has passed over into all men, and is so serious that by it human nature was changed
25 and turned back into inevitable death, are found (as I have already explained) a plurality of sins, besides those others of the parents which, though they cannot to that extent cause a change of nature, yet do involve the children in guilt, unless God's undeserved grace and mercy come to the rescue.

[1] Ex. 20. 5; Deut. 5. 9.   [2] Ezek. 18. 2 ff.   [3] Ps. 51. 5.

THE BAPTISM OF CHRIST BY JOHN

49. For there was no question of being born again in the case of those baptized with the baptism of John, by whom Christ himself was baptized: but as it were by the fore-runner's ministry of that one who said *Prepare the way for the Lord*,[1] they were being prepared for this one only in whom alone they could be born again. For this one's baptism is not in water only as John's was, but also in the Holy Spirit besides:[2] with the result that all who believe in Christ are made regenerate of that same Spirit of whom Christ was so generated as to need no regeneration. For which reason that utterance of the Father which was made over him when baptized, *To-day have I begotten thee*,[3] refers not to that day of time on which he was baptized but to the day of change-less eternity, that he might make it clear that that humanity pertains to the Person of the Only-begotten: for where a day neither begins with the end of yesterday nor ends with the beginning of to-morrow, it is always to-day. So, then, it was his good pleasure to be baptized by John, not that any iniquity of his might be washed away, but so as to set forth his great humility. In fact, baptism found in him nothing to wash away, precisely as death found nothing to punish: so that the devil, conquered and defeated by truth of righteous-ness and not by violence of power, should, for having most unjustly slain him without any sin to deserve it, through him most righteously be deprived of those whom, with sin to deserve it, he was keeping in bondage. Both of these then, both baptism and death, were accepted by him with a definite purpose in view, not of pitiful necessity but rather of pitying good will, so that one Man might take away the sin of the world precisely as one man brought sin into the world, that is, into the entire human race.

[1] Isa. 40. 3; Mark 1. 3; John 1. 23.   [2] Mark 1. 8.
[3] Ps. 2. 7; Luke 3. 22.

Christ is neither more nor less than the similitude of Christ's
death, and the death of Christ crucified neither more nor less
than the similitude of the remission of sin; with the result
that, as in him there took place a real death, so in us there
10 occurs a real remission of sins; and as in him a real resurrection, so in us a real justification. For he says, *What shall we
say, then? Shall we abide in sin, that grace may abound?* [1]
For he had observed previously, *For where sin abounded, there
did grace superabound*: [2] and consequently he proposed to
15 himself the question whether, for the purpose of obtaining
the abundance of grace, one ought to abide in sin. But his
answer was,[3] *God forbid*: and he added, *If we have died to sin,
how shall we have life in it?* And then, to show that we have
died to sin, he says, *Or are ye ignorant that all we who have been
20 baptized in Christ Jesus have been baptized in his death?* If then
it is here shown that we have died to sin because we have
been baptized in the death of Christ, evidently also infants
who are baptized in Christ die to sin because they are
baptized in his death: for with no exception was the
25 observation made, *All we who have been baptized in Christ
Jesus have been baptized in his death,* and the purpose of the
observation was to prove that we have died to sin. But to
what sin do infants die by being born again, except that which
they have contracted by being born? And consequently
30 what follows applies to them as well, *So then we have been
buried together with him by baptism unto death, that like as Christ
has risen from the dead by the glory of the Father, so we also should
walk in newness of life. For if we have been made to be planted
together with the likeness of his death, we shall along with him
35 belong to the resurrection, knowing this, that our old man has been
crucified along with him, that the body of sin may be made void,
that we should no longer be in servitude to sin. For he who has
died is justified from sin. But as we have died with Christ, we*

---

[1] Rom. 6. 1.   [2] Rom. 5. 20.   [3] Rom. 6. 2 ff.

believe that we shall also be alive together with him, knowing that
Christ, on rising from the dead, dieth no more: death hath no 40
further domination over him. For in that he died, he died to sin
once for all: but in that he is alive, he is alive to God. Likewise
ye also must bear in mind that ye have indeed died to sin, but are
alive to God in Christ Jesus. From this then he had taken in
hand to prove that we ought not to abide in sin so that grace 45
may abound, and had asked, If we have died to sin, how shall
we have life in it? And to show that we have died to sin,
he had added, Or are ye ignorant that all we who have been
baptized in Christ Jesus have been baptized in his death? Thus
he has concluded the whole passage in accordance with its 50
beginning. In fact he introduced the death of Christ in such
terms as to suggest that even he had died to sin. To what
sin, unless it means the flesh, in which was not sin but the
likeness of sin, for which reason it is spoken of by the term
" sin "? And so, speaking to those baptized in the death of 55
Christ (and in this not only older persons, but also infants,
are baptized), he says, Likewise ye also—that is, in the same
manner as Christ—likewise must ye also bear in mind that ye have
died to sin, but are alive to God in Christ Jesus.

CHRIST'S SAVING ACTS ARE A PICTURE OF THE
CHRISTIAN LIFE

53. Everything then that was done in respect of the cross
of Christ, his burial, his resurrection on the third day, his
ascension into heaven, his seat at the right hand of the Father,
was so done that in these facts not merely spoken in parables
but actually done, we might have a picture of the Christian 5
life which is being lived here and now. For in respect of
his cross was the observation, But those who belong to Jesus
Christ have crucified their flesh along with the passions and lusts: [1]

[1] Gal. 5. 24.

in respect of his burial, *For we have been buried together with*
10 *Christ by means of baptism, unto death*: [1] in respect of his
resurrection, *That like as Christ has risen again from the dead
by the glory of the Father, so we also should walk in newness of
life*: and in respect of his ascension into heaven and his seat
at the right hand of the Father, *But if ye have risen again with*
15 *Christ, seek the things which are above, where Christ is, sitting
at the right hand of God: set your mind on the things above, not
the things upon earth: for ye have died, and your life is hid with
Christ in God.*[2]

CHRIST'S COMING TO JUDGEMENT

54. Moreover that part of our confession concerning Christ
which refers to the future, namely that he is to come from
heaven to judge the quick and the dead, does not belong to
our life which is being lived here and now, because it is not
5 among the acts which he has done, but among those which
are to be done at the end of the age.   To this subject belongs
the remark the apostle added next, *When Christ, your life,
shall appear, then shall ye also appear along with him in glory.*[3]

"THE QUICK AND THE DEAD"

55. Now the statement that he will judge the quick and
the dead can be taken in two ways: either that we should
understand by "quick" that his coming will find here people
not yet dead but still alive in this flesh, and by "dead" those
5 who have departed or are to depart from the body before he
comes: or by "quick" the righteous, and by "dead"
the unrighteous, seeing that the righteous too will be judged.
For sometimes the judgement of God is set down in respect
of evil, concerning which there is this text, *But those that have*

[1] Rom. 6. 4.   [2] Col. 3. 1.   [3] Col. 3. 4.

done evil, unto the resurrection of judgement : [1] sometimes also in 10
respect of good, according to the saying, *Save me, O God,*
for thy name's sake, and judge me in thy strength.[2]   In fact it
is by the judgement of God that discernment is made of the
good and the evil, that the good may be set apart on the
right hand, to be delivered from evil and not to be destroyed 15
with the evil.[3]   Hence the psalmist's cry, *Judge me, O God.*
And, as it were explaining what he meant, he adds, *And*
discern my cause concerning the unholy nation.[4]

THE HOLY SPIRIT AND THE CHURCH

56. Having treated of Jesus Christ the only Son of God, XV
our Lord, as fully as the brevity of a creed permits, we add
that we also believe in the Holy Ghost, and thus make full
mention of that Trinity which God is.   After that, mention
is made of the holy Church : whereby we are given to under- 5
stand that, after the commemoration of the Creator (that is,
that most supreme Trinity), subsequent reference had to be
made to the rational creation which appertains to Jerusalem
which is free : for all that has been set down with reference
to Christ as man, appertains to the unity of the Person of the 10
Only-begotten.   Thus the correct order of the Creed
demanded that to the Trinity should be subjoined the
Church, as one might say, to the Inhabitant his own house,
to God his own temple, to the Founder his own city.   And
the Church must here be understood in its fullness—not only 15
of that part which is in exile on earth, from the rising of the
sun unto its going down praising the Name of the Lord,[5]
and after the end of its ancient captivity singing a new song,[6]
but also of that part which always since its foundation has in
heaven adhered to God nor has experienced any fall to do it 20

[1] John 5. 29.   [2] Ps. 54. 1.   [3] Cf. Matt. 25. 34.
[4] Ps. 43. 1.   [5] Cf. Ps. 113. 3.   [6] Cf. Ps. 33. 3.

injury. This, among the holy angels, continues always in
blessedness, and to that part of itself which is in exile gives
succour such as is due: because both are destined to be one
in the fellowship of eternity, as it is already one in the bond of
25 charity, seeing it was founded in its wholeness for the worship
of the one God. Therefore neither the whole nor any part
of it desires to be worshipped instead of God, or to stand as
a god to anyone who pertains to that temple of God which
is being builded up of those who are made gods by the
30 God who is not made.[1] Consequently, if the Holy Spirit
were a creature and not the Creator, he would certainly be
a rational creature (for the rational creature is the most
supreme creature): and in that case his position in the Rule
of the Faith would not be before the Church, in that he too
35 would pertain to the Church in respect of that part of it which
is in heaven. Nor would he have a temple, but rather would
himself be a temple. But he has a temple, that of which
the apostle remarks, *Know ye not that* your bodies are *a temple
of the Holy Spirit who is in you, whom ye have from God?*[2]
40 And of these bodies he remarks in another place, *Know ye not
that your bodies are members of Christ?*[3] So then the Holy
Spirit must be God, for he has a temple: and he cannot be
inferior to Christ, whose members he has for his temple.
For there are not two temples, one his, and the other God's:
45 for the same apostle says, *Know ye not that ye are the temple of
God?*, and in proof of this he added, *And that the Spirit of
God dwelleth in you?*[4] So then it is God who is dwelling in
his own temple—not the Holy Spirit only, but also the
Father, and the Son too: and the Son also, referring to his
50 own body through which he has been made the head of the
Church which is among men (so that in all things he might
have the pre-eminence)[5] says, *Destroy this temple, and in*

[1] Cf. Ps. 82. 6.   [2] 1 Cor. 6. 19.   [3] 1 Cor. 6. 15.
[4] 1 Cor. 3. 16.   [5] Cf. Col. 1. 18.

three days I will raise it up.[1]   So then the temple of God, that is, of that whole supreme Trinity, is the holy Church, the Church universal in heaven and in earth.   55

THE CHURCH IN HEAVEN

57. But concerning that which is in heaven, we can make no statement but this, that since the time when *God spared not the angels that sinned* (as the apostle Peter writes) *but cast them down to prisons of the darkness of hell, and delivered them to be reserved for punishment in the judgement,*[2] there is in it none that is 5 evil, neither since then has any fallen nor is to fall.

THE ORDERS OF ANGELS

58. What, however, may be the character of that most blessed and sublime community: what differences of administrations may be there, that though all be called by the generic name of angels (as we read in the Epistle to the Hebrews, *For to which of the angels hath* God *said at any time,* 5 *Sit thou at my right hand ?* [3]—for in such terms as this he has indicated that they are all without exception called angels) yet are there archangels among them: and whether these archangels be called "virtues", so that that may be the meaning of *Praise him, all ye angels of his; praise him, all his* 10 *virtues* [4] (as though we were to put it, "Praise him, all ye angels of his; praise him, all his archangels"): and what may be the distinction between those four terms under which it seems that the apostle embraces that whole celestial community when he says, *Whether thrones or dominations or* 15 *principalities or powers*: [5] these questions let those answer who can, provided they have proof of what they say.   For my part, I admit my ignorance.   Neither have I a certain

---

[1] John 2. 19.   [2] 2 Pet. 2. 4.   [3] Heb. 1. 13.
[4] Ps. 148. 2.   [5] Col. 1. 16.

answer to the question whether to that same community
20 belong the sun and the moon and the rest of the constella-
tions—though some think they are light-bearing bodies,
without either perception or understanding.

THE BODIES ASSUMED BY ANGELS: A NEEDLESS QUESTION

59. Also, who can explain with what quality of bodies
angels have appeared to men, so as not only to be seen but
also to be touched: or at other times with no solid corporeity
but with spiritual potency convey what one may call visions,
5 not to men's bodily eyes, but to their spiritual eyes or (if you
like) their minds: or make communications not to a man's
ear from without but to his soul from within, themselves also
standing within, as is written in the Book of the Prophets,
And the angel who spake in me said unto me [1] (for it does not
10 say "who spake to me", but "in me"): or appear even
in sleep, and converse after the manner of dreams—at all
events we have in the Gospel, *Behold the angel of the Lord
appeared to him in sleep, saying?* [2] For in these ways the
angels seem to indicate that they have not tangible bodies;
15 and they cause it to be a very difficult question how the
patriarchs washed their feet,[3] and how Jacob wrestled with
the angel with so firm a grasp.[4] When these questions are
raised, and each man according to his ability suggests an
answer, the mental exercise is not without its utility, provided
20 the discussion is conducted with moderation and the mistake
is avoided of people supposing they know what they know
not. For what need is there for these and things like these to
be affirmed or denied or defined with precision, when
ignorance of them involves no blame?

[1] Zech. 1. 9.
[2] Matt. 1. 20.
[3] Gen. 18. 4; 19. 2.
[4] Gen. 32. 24.

SATAN TRANSFORMED INTO AN ANGEL OF LIGHT

60. More need is there to adjudicate and discern when it XVI
is that Satan transfigures himself into an angel of light,[1] so
that he may not by deception seduce one to baleful courses.
For when he deceives the senses of the body, yet does not
dislodge the mind from that true and upright judgement 5
by which a man conducts his life in faith, there is no danger
that affects religion: or when, in the pretence of being
good, he either does or says the things which are characteristic
of good angels, even if one supposes him to be good no error
is involved which is perilous or mortal to Christian faith. 10
But when by these means he begins to attract things not his
own to those that are his own, at such times there is cause
for great and necessary diligence, to discern him and not to
follow after him. But how few men are there who are
competent to escape all his pestilent wiles, unless God guide 15
and protect them! Yet the very difficulty of this situation
is to this extent useful, that it precludes any from being his
own hope, or one man another man's hope, making it clear
that God is the hope of all that are his own: for that this is
the rather to our profit no godly man has any doubt.   20

THE CHURCH AT HOME IN HEAVEN, IN EXILE
ON EARTH

61. So, then, this Church which consists in the holy angels
and virtues of God will become known to us in its real
character when we have become united with it unto the end
so as, along with it, to possess everlasting beatitude: whereas
this which is in exile from it on earth is the better known to 5
us in that we are in it, and in that it consists of men, which
we also are. By the blood of the Mediator, himself without

[1] Cf. 2 Cor. ii. 14.

F

sin, this has been redeemed from all sin : and it is this Church which says, *If God be for us, who is against us ? For he hath*
10 *not spared his own Son, but hath delivered him up for us all.*[1] For not for the angels did Christ die.[2] And yet even for the angels is there some advantage in whatever of mankind is by his death redeemed and delivered from evil, because in some sort these are returning into favour with them, having ended
15 the hostilities which sins have caused between mankind and the holy angels, and because from out of men's very redemption the losses caused by that angelic collapse are being repaired.

ALL THINGS ARE BEING RESTORED IN CHRIST

62. No doubt the holy angels are cognizant of the additional numbers the human race must supply to restore the completeness which that city is looking for : they will have obtained their information from God, for in the eternal
5 contemplation of his verity their blessedness has its being. It is in view of this that the apostle says that all things are being restored in Christ, *all things both which are in heaven and which are on earth.*[3] Those in fact which are in heaven are restored when that which fell away in angels is paid back
10 from among men : while those which are on earth are restored when men themselves, those predestined to eternal life, are renewed from the oldness of corruption. In this way that one and only sacrifice in which the Mediator was slain, that one sacrifice prefigured by many offerings in the
15 law, is the means by which heavenly things are made at peace with earthly and earthly things with heavenly. For, as the same apostle affirms, *It was God's good pleasure that in him all fullness should dwell, and that by him all things should be reconciled unto himself (making them at peace by the blood of his cross), both*
20 *those that are on earth and those that are in heaven.*[4]

[1] Rom. 8. 31.   [2] Cf. Heb. 2. 16.   [3] Eph. 1. 10.   [4] Col. 1. 19, 20.

THE PEACE OF GOD WHICH PASSETH ALL
UNDERSTANDING

63. That peace, as the Scripture says, *passeth all under-standing*:[1] we are not competent to know it except when we have attained to it. That the heavenly things should be made at peace can only mean at peace with us, by their being in concord with us. For in heaven there is always peace, the 5 intellectual created beings being without exception at peace both among themselves and with their Creator. This peace, as we have observed, passes all understanding—meaning of course our understanding, not theirs who always behold the Father's face.[2] We, however, great as may be the measure 10 of the human intelligence that is in us, know in part, and see at present through a mirror in an enigma.[3] But when we have been made equal with the angels of God,[4] then we like them shall see face to face, and shall have towards them the same peace which they have towards us, because we shall love 15 them no less than we are now loved by them. Thus will their peace be made known to us, because ours will be of the same quality and depth as theirs, and will no longer pass our understanding: yet will the peace of God, which is already in heaven towards us, surpass both our understanding and theirs: 20 no doubt of it. For every rational creature which is in possession of blessedness is so from him, not he from it. From which it follows that, by a preferable interpretation of the text *The peace of God passeth all understanding*, the expression "all" must be taken as excluding not even the under- 25 standing of the holy angels, but that of God alone: for obviously it is not the case that his peace passes his own understanding.

[1] Phil. 4. 7.
[2] Cf. Matt. 18. 10.
[3] Cf. 1 Cor. 13. 12.
[4] Luke 20. 36.

THE REMISSION OF SINS

XVII 64. Now the angels are in concord with us even in this
present time, so long as our sins are obtaining remission.   For
this reason, in the arrangement of the Creed, the remission of
sins comes after the mention of the holy Church.   For it is
5 by this remission that the Church on earth remains standing :
by it, that that is not being lost which was lost and has been
found.[1]   Leaving out of account the boon of baptism, which
has been bestowed as a remedy for original sin, that that which
was contracted by generation may be abstracted by regenera-
10 tion (yet besides this it also takes away actual sins, all that it
finds to have been committed in thought, word, and deed) :
leaving out of account then this great remission, from which
the renewal of man takes its beginning and in which is paid off
all guilt both ingenerate and acquired, the rest of the life also
15 of those of an age to have the use of reason, however great
the fertility of righteousness in which it excels, is not exempt
from the forgiveness of sins.   For even the sons of God, so
long as they are alive in the midst of death, are in conflict
with death;   and though the word be true that is spoken of
20 them, *As many as are led by the Spirit of God, these are sons of
God*,[2] yet does the stirring of them by the Spirit of God, and
their progress towards God as sons of God, not preclude their
being led by their own spirit, especially as the corruptible
body presses it down;[3] and so, as sons of man, they do in
25 certain human emotions turn aside towards themselves, and
consequently sin.   Yet there are degrees : for it does not
follow that because every crime is a sin, therefore every sin is a
crime.   And so we say that it is possible for the life of saintly
men, even while they are living amidst this death, to be found
30 free from crime : yet that *if we shall say we have no sin*, as that
great apostle puts it, *we deceive ourselves and the truth is not in us*.[4]

[1] Cf. Luke 15. 32.   [2] Rom. 8. 14.   [3] Cf. Wisd. 9. 15.   [4] 1 John 1. 8.

PENANCE

65. Yet not even with regard to these crimes, however serious, and their remission within the holy Church, must we despair of God's mercy towards such as do penance according to the measure of each man's sin.   Though in the doing of penance, where the sin committed is such as even to entail 5 the separation of the sinner from the body of Christ, the thing to be considered is not the reckoning of time, but of sorrow (for, *A contrite and humbled heart God doth not despise* [1]) ; yet because for the most part the sorrow of one man's heart is hidden from the other, and is not brought within others' 10 cognizance by means of speech or any other indications (though it is in full view of him to whom we say, *My groaning is not hid from thee* [2]), with good reason do those in authority over the churches appoint seasons of penance, that satisfaction may also be made to the Church within which the sins receive 15 remission : for outside the Church they have no remission. For it is the Church in particular which has received the earnest, the Holy Spirit,[3] apart from whom no sins receive remission, to the intent that those who have them remitted may obtain eternal life.   20

FORGIVENESS OF SINS HAS IN VIEW THE JUDGEMENT TO COME

66. For remission of sins is primarily practised in view of the judgement to come.   In this life, however, there is such great force in the saying that is written, *An heavy yoke is upon the sons of Adam from the day of exit from their mother's womb even unto the day of burial within the mother of all,* [4] that we 5 observe even infants, after the washing of regeneration,

---

[1] Ps. 51. 17.   [2] Ps. 38. 9.
[3] Cf. 2 Cor. 1. 22.   [4] Ecclus. 40. 1.

tormented by the affliction of divers sorrows: from which
we may understand that all that takes place in the sacraments
of salvation pertains rather to the hope of good things to
10 come than to the retention or acquisition of good things
present. Moreover, in this life many sins appear to be over-
looked and to be visited with no retribution, yet are their
penalties kept in store for the future: for with good reason
is that day in particular called the day of judgement, on which
15 he is to come who is the Judge of the quick and the dead.
On the other hand, some sins here receive retribution, while
yet, if they are forgiven, they will certainly do no harm in
the world to come. For this reason the apostle refers to
certain temporal penalties which, so as not to be kept in
20 store until the end, are during this life imposed on sinners
whose sins are cancelled, and says, *For if we judged ourselves,
we should not be judged by the Lord: but when we are judged by
the Lord we are chastened, that we be not condemned with this
world.*[1]

FAITH, UNLESS IT "WORKETH IN LOVE", IS NOT A SAVING FAITH

XVIII   67. There are some who suppose also that those who
do not abandon the name of Christ, who are baptized in the
Church with his baptism, and are not cut off from the Church
by any schism or heresy, in however great wickedness they
5 live, wickedness which they neither wipe out by penitence
nor pay off by almsgiving, but obstinately persist in it right
to the last day of their life, yet will be saved through fire—
"punished by a fire which, in view of the magnitude of
their crimes and misdeeds, is of long duration, yet is not
10 eternal". Those who suppose so, though they remain
catholics, seem to me to be misled by a sort of human

[1] 1 Cor. 11. 31, 32.

kindliness.   For divine Scripture, on being asked its opinion,
gives a different answer.   But I have written a book on this
question, with the title " Concerning Faith and Works ", in
which, as well as, with God's help, I was able, I have shown 15
according to the Holy Scriptures that men are saved by that
faith to which the apostle Paul gave perfectly clear expression
when he said, *For in Christ Jesus neither circumcision availeth
anything nor uncircumcision, but faith which worketh by affection.*[1]
But if the works it does are bad and not good, it is, as the 20
apostle James says, *dead in itself.*[2]   And James says again, *If
any man say he hath faith, while he hath not works, can faith save
him ?*[3]   So then if a wicked man is to be saved through fire
for the sake of faith alone, and if that is the meaning of the
blessed apostle Paul's statement, *Yet he himself shall be saved,* 25
yet so as through fire,[4] in that case faith without works will have
power to save, and the statement of his fellow-apostle James
will be untrue.   That also will be untrue which Paul himself
has said :   *Be not misled : neither fornicators nor idolaters nor*
adulterers nor effeminate nor abusers of themselves with men, nor 30
thieves nor covetous nor revilers nor drunkards nor extortioners,
shall obtain possession of the kingdom of God.[5]   If, however,
while persisting in these crimes, they are for all that to be saved
because of the faith of Christ, how can they fail to be in the
kingdom of God?
                                                                35

" SHALL BE SAVED, SO AS THROUGH FIRE "

68. Seeing, however, that such clear and evident apostolic
testimonies as these cannot be untrue, that other obscure
statement made with reference to those who build, upon the
foundation which is Christ, neither gold nor silver nor
precious stones, but wood, hay, and stubble (for it is of these 5

[1] Gal. 5. 6.   [2] Jas. 2. 17.   [3] Jas. 2. 14.
[4] 1 Cor. 3. 15.   [5] 1 Cor. 6. 9, 10.

that the statement is made that they will be saved through
fire, because the goodness of the foundation will preclude
their perishing) [1] must be interpreted in such a manner as not
to be found in contradiction with these statements that are
10 not obscure. Wood and hay and stubble may without
incongruity be taken as the sort of desires for the things of
this world, things perfectly legitimate in themselves, which
yet cannot be relinquished without regret. When, however, such regret is as a fire, yet in the man's heart Christ has
15 his position as foundation (that is, so that nothing is given
preference over him), and the man who is on fire with that
regret would rather be deprived of the things he so loves than
be deprived of Christ, he would be saved through fire. But
if in time of temptation his preference has been to retain this
20 kind of temporal and worldly thing rather than Christ, he
has not had Christ at his foundation: for he has had these
things in the prior place, though in a building there is nothing
prior to the foundation. For the fire to which the apostle
referred in that passage must be interpreted as of such a nature
25 that both persons pass through it, the one who builds upon
this foundation gold, silver, and precious stones, as well as he
who builds wood, hay, and stubble. For the apostle
continued: *The fire shall try every man's work, of what kind
it is: if any man's work shall abide, which he hath built thereupon,*
30 *he shall receive a reward: but if any man's work shall be burned
up, he shall suffer loss; but he himself shall be saved, yet so as
through fire.* [2] It is not then the work of one of them, but of
each one, that the fire shall try. One sort of fire is the
temptation of affliction, of which it is plainly written in
35 another passage: *The furnace proveth the potter's vessels, and
just men the temptation of affliction.* [3] Such fire has during this
passing life the effect the apostle referred to if it comes upon

[1] Cf. 1 Cor. 3. 11 ff.   [2] 1 Cor. 3. 13–15.
[3] Cf. Ecclus. 27. 5 and 2. 5.

two of the faithful, one of whom is thinking upon the things
which are God's, how he may please God, is building in fact,
upon Christ as foundation, gold, silver, and precious stones; 40
while the other is thinking upon the things which are the
world's, how he may please his wife,[1] is in fact building,
upon the same foundation, wood, hay, and stubble. The
work of the one is not burned up, because he has not set his
affections upon things which it distresses him to lose. The 45
other's work, however, is burned up, because the loss of
such things as human love values must needs be grievous:
yet because, when choice between the two is set before him,
he prefers to be deprived of the other things, and not of
Christ, and does not apostatize from Christ for fear of losing 50
those, in spite of his grief at losing them, he himself is saved,
yet so as through fire: for he is burned with sorrow at the
loss of the things he has set his affections upon, yet is not
overthrown nor burned away, being protected by the
firmness and indestructibility of his foundation.   55

PERHAPS SOME WILL BE SAVED THROUGH
A SORT OF FIRE

69. It is not beyond belief that something of the sort takes
place even after this life, and there is room for inquiry
whether it is so, and the answer may be found (or not found)
to be that a certain number of the faithful are the more
belatedly or the more speedily saved, through a sort of fire, 5
the more they have or the less they have set their affections
on the good things that perish: not, however, those of
whom the pronouncement was made that *they shall not
obtain possession of the kingdom of God*,[2] unless, on their doing
appropriate penance, those crimes are forgiven them. By 10
" appropriate " I mean that they be not unfruitful in alms-

---

[1] Cf. 1 Cor. 7. 32, 33.   [2] 1 Cor. 6. 10.

giving: for to it divine Scripture has assigned so high a value
that our Lord declares that it is simply and solely with the
fruit of it that he will credit those on his right hand, and
15 simply and solely with unfruitfulness in it that he will dis-
credit those on his left, when he says to the former, *Come, ye
blessed of my Father, receive the kingdom*; and to the latter,
Depart, ye cursed, into eternal fire.[1]

ALMSGIVING CONVEYS NO LICENCE TO SIN

XIX   70. Of course we must take care that no one should think
that those outrageous crimes, the commission of which
excludes from possession of the kingdom of God, may be
perpetrated every day, and every day bought off by alms-
5 giving. Rather should there take place an amendment of
life: and by means of almsgiving God should be brought to
pardon sins past, and not in some sort of way bribed to allow
them to be continually committed with impunity. For
to no man hath he given licence to sin,[2] albeit by showing mercy
10 he blots out sins already committed, provided appropriate
satisfaction be not neglected.

PRAYER CONVEYS FORGIVENESS FOR TRIVIAL SINS

71. But for those daily short-lived and trivial sins from
which this life is never exempt, the daily prayer of the
faithful is sufficient satisfaction. For the right to say *Our
Father which art in heaven* [3] belongs to such as are already born
5 again to a heavenly Father, of water and the Spirit. This
prayer altogether wipes out those little daily sins. It also
wipes out those from which the life of believers, wicked
though it may have been, is separating itself by a penitential
change for the better, provided that the earnestness of the
10 petition *Forgive us our debts* (for there always are debts to be

[1] Matt. 25. 31–46.   [2] Ecclus. 15. 20.   [3] Matt. 6. 9.

forgiven) is balanced by the earnestness of the statement,
As we also forgive our debtors—provided, that is, that we are
doing as we say we are: for it is an act of alms-giving to
forgive a fellow man who asks for pardon.

VARIOUS SORTS OF ALMSGIVING

72. For this reason, our Lord's saying, *Give alms, and
behold all things are clean unto you*,[1] is valid in respect of all
acts done through helpful compassion. Alms therefore are
given, not only by him who gives food to the hungry, drink
to the thirsty, clothing to the naked, lodging to the stranger, 5
refuge to the fugitive, visitation to the sick or imprisoned,
redemption to the captive, support to the weakling, leading
to the blind, consolation to the sorrowful, healing to the
unhealthy, direction to the erring, counsel to the doubtful,
and any necessary thing to him that is in need of it, but also 10
by him who gives pardon to the sinner. Also, he who
corrects with the rod, or constrains by any sort of discipline,
him over whom he has authority, while yet forgiving from
the heart the sin by which he has been injured or offended,
or who prays for him to be forgiven, is giving alms not only 15
by the fact of forgiving and praying but also by the act of
rebuking or of inflicting on him some corrective penalty;
the reason being that he is showing compassion. For often-
times benefits are conferred upon those who have no wish
for them, as when the benefactor consults not their will 20
but their profit: because it appears that they are their own
worst enemies, while their friends are those whom they
regard as enemies, to whom in error they return evil for good,
though a Christian ought not even to return evil for evil.
Thus there are many sorts of almsgiving, by the performance of 25
which we are assisted towards having our own sins forgiven.

[1] Luke 11. 41.

THE BEST ALMSGIVING IS TO FORGIVE OTHERS

73. But there is nothing which surpasses that alms-doing by which we forgive from the heart another man's sins against us. For it is an easier thing for you to be well disposed, or even generous, towards one who has done you 5 no harm. The other is much nobler, a matter of magnificent generosity, for you to love even your own enemy, and always to wish well, and to do what good you can, to one who wishes you ill, and does it if he can, while you listen to God saying, *Love your enemies, do good to them that hate you, and* 10 *pray for them that persecute you.*[1] But seeing that these acts are characteristic of the perfect sons of God—an ideal towards which it is every faithful person's duty to hasten, training his human mind to this attitude by prayer to God and by reasoning and wrestling with himself—yet in that such 15 nobility of character can hardly be expected of all those great congregations whose prayers we suppose are heard when in the Lord's Prayer they say, *Forgive us our debts, as we also forgive our debtors,*[2] we may presume that the letter of this bargain is kept if a man who has not yet progressed so far as 20 to love his enemy, does for all that, when asked for forgiveness by a man who has sinned against him, forgive him from his heart: because evidently he too wishes to be forgiven on request when he says in his prayer, *As we also forgive our debtors,* meaning "Forgive us our debts at our request, just as 25 we also forgive our debtors at their request".

THERE IS NO FORGIVENESS FOR THE UNFORGIVING

74. Moreover, if the person who makes this request of the man against whom he has sinned is moved by his own sin to make the request, he is no longer to be reckoned an

[1] Matt. 5. 44.   [2] Matt. 6. 12.

enemy: so there will be no difficulty in loving him, as there
was while he was actively hostile. But no one who refuses 5
to forgive from the heart a person who does ask and is
repentant of his sin, must ever think his own sins are forgiven
by the Lord: for the Truth is incapable of lying. Yet is
there any hearer or reader of the Gospel who does not know
who it was that said, *I am the truth*? [1] The same who, having 10
set out the words of the prayer, strongly reinforced this
particular sentence of it, in the words: *For if ye forgive men
their sins, your heavenly Father will also forgive you your offences:
but if ye forgive not men, neither will your Father forgive you your
sins.* [2] Anyone who does not awake at this mighty thunder 15
is not asleep but dead: yet God is able even to raise up the
dead.

ALMSGIVING CONVEYS NO FORGIVENESS FOR THE UNREGENERATE

75. Of course those whose life is outrageously wicked, XX
and who have no interest in amending their life and manners,
yet in the midst of their wickednesses and excesses cease not
to exercise themselves in almsgiving, are unjustified in any
self-approbation on the ground that our Lord said, *Give* 5
alms, and behold all things are clean unto you. [3] They fail to
understand the full bearing of this remark. If they wish to
understand, let them note to whom it was addressed. They
may learn it from the Gospel, as follows: *While he was
speaking, a certain Pharisee asked him to dine with him. And he* 10
*went in, and sat down. The Pharisee, however, began to reason
within himself, saying, Why did he not wash before dinner?
And the Lord said unto him, Now do ye Pharisees cleanse the
outside of the cup and the dish: but what is within you is full of
rapine and iniquity. Ye fools: did not he that made that which is* 15

[1] John 14. 6.   [2] Matt. 6. 14, 15.   [3] Luke 11. 41.

without make also that which is within? [*See to it that that which is within also be made clean.*] *And, for the rest, give alms, and behold all things are clean unto you.*[1] Are we to interpret this as if the Pharisees, who had not the faith of Christ, were,
20 without any need for believing in him or for being born again of water and the Spirit, going to find all things clean to them solely by their giving alms, as the people we are speaking of suppose they should be given? Of course not, seeing that all are unclean who are not cleansed by the faith
25 of Christ, of which it is written, *Cleansing their hearts by faith,*[2] and seeing that the apostle says, *But to the unclean and disbelieving nothing is clean, but both their mind and conscience are polluted.*[3] How then could all have been clean to the Pharisees if they gave alms while they continued disbelieving?
30 And how could they have been believers when they had refused to believe in Christ and to be born again in his grace? And yet it was the truth that was told them, *Give alms, and behold all things are clean unto you.*

ALMSGIVING BEGINS WITH ONESELF

76. The explanation is that anyone who proposes to give alms in proper order must begin with himself, giving alms to himself first of all. For almsgiving is a work of mercy, and there is supreme truth in the saying, *Have mercy on thine own*
5 *soul and please God.*[4] This, the desire of pleasing God, is the reason why we are born again: for he is rightly displeased with the taint we contracted on being born. This is our first act of almsgiving: and we have done it to ourselves, in that when we were in misery we sought and found our-
10 selves by the mercy of God who showeth mercy, while we acknowledged his righteous judgement by which we were

---

[1] Luke 11. 37–41.
[2] Acts 15. 9.
[3] Titus 1. 15.
[4] Cf. Ecclus. 30. 23.

cast into misery (the judgement of which the apostle observes, *Judgement indeed was of one unto condemnation* [1]) and gave thanks to his great charity (of which the same preacher of grace remarks, *But God commendeth his own affection in us in that, though we were yet sinners, Christ died for us* [2]), with the result that we also, passing true judgement on our own misery, and loving God with the charity which is his own gift to us, are living a pious and upright life. It was because the Pharisees were neglecting this judgement and charity of God, that for the sake of the almsgiving which they practised they made a tithe even of the very smallest of their produce, yet failed to make their almsgiving begin with themselves and to show mercy upon themselves first of all. This order of affection is the reason for the saying, *Thou shalt love thy neighbour as thyself.* [3] So then, having rebuked them for washing themselves on the outside while within they were full of rapine and iniquity, he admonishes them that there is a certain sort of almsgiving which a man owes as a gift to himself in the first instance, and by which the things within are made clean: *And, for the rest, give alms, and behold all things are clean unto you.* [4] And then, to show what his admonition meant, and what it was that they were neglecting to do, and to avoid the impression that he was unaware of the alms they gave, he says, *But woe unto you Pharisees*, as though he were to say, "Now I have given you an injunction as to the giving of the alms by which all things may be clean unto you, but woe unto you, *who tithe mint and rue and every herb*: for I know of these alms of yours, lest you should suppose it is of them that I have just admonished you: *and neglect the judgement and charity of God,* [5] the alms by which you could be made clean from every internal defilement, so that even your bodies which you do wash would be clean "—

[1] Rom. 5. 16.   [2] Rom. 5. 8.   [3] Lev. 19. 18; Luke 10. 27.
[4] Luke 11. 41.   [5] Luke 11. 42.

for this is the meaning of " all ", namely things within and
45 things without, as we read elsewhere, *Cleanse the things
which are within, and the things which are without will be clean.*[1]
But that he might not have the appearance of rejecting those
alms which are done of the fruits of the earth, he adds, *These
ought ye to have done,* that is, judgement and the charity of
50 God, *and not to leave the other undone,*[2] meaning alms of the
fruits of their fields.

ALMSGIVING CONVEYS NO IMPUNITY TO SIN

77. So let those be undeceived who suppose that by any
abundance of alms of their produce, or of any amount of
money, they are purchasing indulgence to continue in the
outrageousness of their crimes or the wickedness of their
5 misdeeds. For not only do they do these things, but they are
so attached to them as to hope always to be immersed in
them, provided they can do so with impunity. But *he that
loveth iniquity hateth his own soul* :[3] and the man who hates
his own soul is not merciful towards it, but ruthless. In-
10 deed in loving it according to the world, he hates it according
to God. If then it were his wish to do it an alms by which
all things should be clean to him, he would hate it according
to the world and love it according to God. But no man
ever gives any alms at all unless he receive from him who
15 has need of nothing the store from which to give it : and
that is the reason behind, *His mercy shall anticipate me.*[4]

THE DISTINCTION OF LIGHT AND GRAVE SINS IS A
MATTER FOR DIVINE JUDGEMENT

XXI   78. But the weighing up of which are light and which are
grave sins is a matter not for human but for divine judge-

---

[1] Cf. Matt. 23. 26.   [2] Luke 11. 42.
[3] Prov. 8. 36.   [4] LXX Ps. 58. 11 (59. 10).

ment. For we notice that some have been permitted by way of indulgence by no less people than the apostles, as for example the advice which the revered apostle Paul gives to husbands and wives: *Defraud not one another, unless it be by consent, for a time, that ye may give yourselves to prayer; and so must ye come together again, lest Satan tempt you because of your incontinency.*[1] Now this might have been supposed to be no sin, I mean, to have conjugal intercourse not for the purpose of begetting children (which is the benefit of matrimony) but even for the sake of carnal pleasure, so that the weakness of the incontinent may avoid the deadly evil of fornication or adultery or some other uncleanness which it is a shame even to speak of, and to which passion may drag people by the tempting of Satan. This might then, I repeat, have been supposed to be no sin, if he had omitted to add, *But this I say by way of indulgence, not of commandment.*[2] Will anyone now deny that it is a sin, after admitting that by apostolic authority indulgence is granted to those who practise it? Something similar arises when he says, *Dare any of you, having a matter against another, go to law before the unrighteous, and not before the saints?*[3] And shortly afterwards, *If then ye have judgements of things pertaining to this world, set those to judge who are disesteemed in the church. I speak to your shame. Is it so, that there is not among you any that is wise, that is competent to judge between his brethren, but brother goeth to law with brother, and this before unbelievers?*[4] Here too it might have been supposed that it is no sin to have a lawsuit against another, but merely to consent to have judgement given outside the Church, if he had not continued: *Now indeed it is altogether a sin that ye have lawsuits between you.*[5] And that no one might find excuses for this by saying that he had a just case, and was suffering an injustice which he desired to be relieved

[1] I Cor. 7. 5.   [2] I Cor. 7. 6.   [3] I Cor. 6. 1.
[4] I Cor. 6. 4–6.   [5] I Cor. 6. 7.

G

35 of by the judgement of the court, the apostle at once meets
such excuses, whether tacit or expressed, with the words,
*Why do ye not rather put up with the injustice ? Why do ye
not rather let yourselves be wronged ?*   And thus we come back
to what our Lord said, *If any man will take thy coat*, and will
40 contend with thee in judgement, *let him have thy cloak also* : [1]
and, in another place, *Of him that taketh away thy goods, ask
them not again.*[2] Thus he forbade his disciples to have a
lawsuit with other men respecting secular matters : and in
accordance with this teaching the apostle says it is a sin.   Yet
45 when he permits such suits to be concluded in the Church
among the brethren, with brethren for judges, while outside
the Church he stringently forbids it, it is clear in this case as
well what concession is made to the weak by way of
indulgence.   On account of sins of this sort, and others no
50 doubt less than these, which are committed through our
offending in words and thoughts (as the apostle James admits
when he says, *For in many things we all offend*)[3], we are called
upon daily and frequently to pray to the Lord saying *Forgive
us our debts*, without departing from the truth in what comes
55 after, *As we also forgive our debtors.*[4]

SOME APPARENTLY TRIVIAL SINS ARE SERIOUS

79. Yet there are some sins which might have been
supposed quite trivial unless they were proved in the
Scriptures to be more serious than we thought.   For who
would have supposed that a man who said to his brother
5 " Thou fool " was in danger of hell, unless he who is the
Truth had said so ? [5]   To this wound, however, he immediately applied a remedy when he added the precept of
brotherly reconciliation.   At any rate, he said next, *Therefore*

[1] Matt. 5. 40.   [2] Luke 6. 30.   [3] Jas. 3. 2.
[4] Matt. 6. 12.   [5] Matt. 5. 22.

if thou shalt be offering thy gift at the altar, and there shalt remember
that thy brother hath somewhat against thee, and so on.[1]   Or 10
who would guess what a great sin it is to observe days and
months and years and seasons [2] (as those do who on specified
days or months or years consent or refuse to begin some
undertaking, on the ground that, following the vain teachings
of men, they take account of lucky or unlucky seasons), if 15
we did not measure the enormity of this evil by the apostle's
fear, when he says to such people, *I fear you, lest perchance to*
no purpose I have laboured among you? [3]

USE AND HABIT CAUSE SERIOUS SINS TO
SEEM TRIVIAL

80. To make matters worse, it comes about that sins in
themselves very great and horrible, when they have become
habitual, give the impression of being either small ones or not
sins at all : to such an extent that, far from seeing any need
to hide them, people think they should even be advertised and 5
broadcast, since, as the Scripture puts it, *The wicked is praised*
in his own soul's desires, and he that doeth iniquity is spoken
well of.[4]   Iniquity like this is in the Scriptures described as
"a cry", as you have it in the prophet Isaiah of the unfruitful vineyard, *I looked that it should do judgement, but it did* 10
iniquity, not righteousness but a cry.[5]   To this cry refers the
text of Genesis, *The cry of Sodom and Gomorrah is become very*
great,[6] because not only were those wickednesses exempt
from punishment, but they were even publicly practised as
by law.   So in our times too, such a number of sins, though 15
not as bad as these, have now become such a matter of open
habit that we dare not because of them excommunicate any
layman, or even depose a cleric.   For this reason, when, a

---

[1] Matt. 5. 23.   [2] Cf. Gal. 4. 10.   [3] Gal. 4. 11.
[4] Ps. 10. 3.   [5] Isa. 5. 7.   [6] Gen. 18. 20.

few years ago, I was expounding the Epistle to the Galatians,
20 on that very passage where the apostle says, *I fear you, lest
perchance to no purpose I have laboured among you,*[1] I was
constrained to cry out: " Woe to the sins of men, for it is
only when they are unusual that we are aghast at them :
while as for the usual ones, for the washing away of which
25 the blood of the Son of God was shed, although they are so
serious as to cause the kingdom of God to be entirely shut
against them, by often seeing them we are impelled to tolerate
them all, and by often tolerating them are brought even to
commit some of them. And would to God we did not
30 practise all those we have found ourselves unable to
prevent ! " I wonder whether sorrow beyond measure
constrained me to speak over-hastily.

OF IGNORANCE AND FRAILTY, AND THE NEED FOR
DIVINE AID

XXII   81. I am going to repeat now a statement I have frequently
made elsewhere in my treatises : The causes of our sinning
are twofold, either that we do not perceive what we ought
to do, or that we fail to do what we are already aware ought
5 to be done. The former of these is the sin of ignorance, the
latter of frailty. Against these it is our duty to fight. Yet
we certainly get the worst of it unless we have the help of
God, not only to see what ought to be done, but also that, as
we recover our health, the delights of righteousness may
10 overcome in us the delights of those things which we desire
to have or else fear to lose, and in consequence continue to
sin in spite of full knowledge and perception : so that we are
no longer merely sinners (this we were even when we sinned
through ignorance) but also transgressors of the law, seeing
15 we are leaving that undone which we know ought to be

[1] Gal. 4. 11.

done, or even doing that which we know ought not to be done. Consequently not only if we have sinned must he be asked for pardon (that is why we say, *Forgive us our debts, as we also forgive our debtors*), but also to keep us from sinning he must be asked to guide us (which is why we say, *Lead us not into temptation*) : [1] he must be asked, I say, to whom we say in the psalm, *The Lord is my light and my healing*,[2] so that the light may strip us of our ignorance, the healing strip us of our frailty.

OF THOSE WHO NEGLECT TO DO PENANCE

82. For it frequently happens that, when there is reasonable cause according to church custom for penance to be done, through frailty it fails to be done: for there is a cowardly fear of being disapproved of, while people take more delight in men's esteem than in the righteousness by which a man humbles himself in doing penance. Therefore God's mercy is needed not only while penance is being done, but also that it may be done: otherwise the apostle would not have said of some, *Lest peradventure God grant them repentance*.[3] And, to explain Peter's weeping bitterly, we have the evangelist's previous statement that the Lord looked upon him.[4]

THE SIN AGAINST THE HOLY GHOST

83. He however who, refusing to believe that sins are forgiven in the Church, despises this great bounty of God's munificence, and continues in this obstinacy of mind right to the day of his death, is guilty of that unforgivable sin against the Holy Spirit in whom Christ grants forgiveness of sins. This difficult question I have discussed as convincingly as I was able in a book written for that express purpose.

[1] Matt. 6. 12, 13.   [2] Ps. 27. 1.
[3] 2 Tim. 2. 25.   [4] Cf. Luke 22. 61.

QUESTIONS CONCERNING THE RESURRECTION

XXIII   84. Now concerning the resurrection of the flesh—not as some have been brought to life again and a second time have died, but the resurrection to eternal life, as the flesh of Christ himself rose again—I do not see how I can discuss this with
5 brevity while yet doing justice to all the questions which are customarily raised about this subject.   However, no Christian must have any doubt that there is to be a resurrection of the flesh of all men who have been or are to be born, who have died or are to die.

UNTIMELY BIRTHS

85. In the first place a question arises on this subject concerning miscarriages, children born so to speak in their mother's womb, but without a chance of being born again. If we express the view that they will rise again, the idea is at
5 least tolerable in the case of those which have attained complete development.   But as for undeveloped miscarriages, surely one would be more inclined to suspect that they come to nothing, as does the seed which fails of conception.   Also no one will dare to deny, even though one dare not affirm, that
10 the effect of the resurrection will be that anything lacking to full development will be supplied, and thus they will not lack the perfection which time would have brought, as also they will not have the blemishes which time had brought.   Thus neither in respect of that fitness and propriety which the
15 months would have added will nature suffer loss, nor in respect of those opposite and contrary qualities which the months had added will nature be defaced.   Rather will there be a perfecting of what was not yet perfect, as there will be a restoration of what had become blemished.

ALL THAT HAVE ONCE LIVED WILL PARTAKE OF
THE RESURRECTION

86. For this reason there is room for inquiry and discussion among the learned, so long as they do it with delicacy, regarding a question to which I am not sure that man can find the answer: at what point does the human being begin to be alive in the womb, and is there even a sort of concealed 5 life when it is not as yet made evident by the movements of the living child? For it seems an excessive presumption to deny that there has been life in the case of births which are dissected limb by limb and ejected from the wombs of pregnant women so that they may not, by being left there 10 dead, cause the death of their mothers as well. However that may be, immediately a human being begins to have life, certainly from then on he is capable of dying: and I cannot imagine how a dead person, at whatever point it has been possible for death to overtake him, can fail to have a part in 15 the resurrection of the dead.

OF MONSTROSITIES

87. Moreover even monstrosities, such as are born and have life, however soon they die, will certainly rise again: yet it must not be supposed they will rise again in that form, but rather with their nature rectified and corrected. For God forbid that that child with two sets of everything who 5 was born recently in the East, about whom we have been told by brethren well worthy of credence who actually saw him, and about whom Jerome the presbyter, of holy memory, has left a writing—God forbid, I say, that we should suppose that he will rise again as two men in one, and not rather as 10 two men, as would have been the case if it had been twins that were born. So also the rest which, though born one at

a time, yet are termed monstrosities, because they have something excessive or something defective or are marked by
15 some unusual deformity, will be recalled at the resurrection
to the true shape of human nature. Thus each individual
soul will possess its own individual body: even those that
were born adhering together will no longer adhere, but each
individual will be separately equipped with those limbs of
20 his own of which the undefective human body is constructed.

THE WHOLE FLESH WILL BE RESTORED AGAIN

88. For the earthy matter of which mortals' flesh is created
is never lost to God: but into whatsoever dust or ashes it be
dissolved, into whatsoever vapours or mists it flee away,
into whatsoever substance of other bodies it be converted,
5 or even into the very elements, into whatsoever animals' or
men's food it be reduced, so as to be changed into their flesh,
it returns in a moment of time to that human soul which in
the first place made it animate, and caused it to become a
human being, to have life, and to grow.

GOD'S CARE WILL PRECLUDE ANYTHING UNSEEMLY

89. So this earthy matter, which at the soul's departure
becomes a corpse, will not at the resurrection be so reconstructed that those elements which decay away and suffer
conversion into successive forms and shapes of other entities
5 (albeit they do return to the body from which they have
decayed) must of necessity come back to the same parts of
the body in which they were before. Otherwise, if the hair
of the head receives back again all that has been cut off in
frequent trimmings, if the finger-nails get back what repeated
10 cutting has taken away, this excess becomes an ugliness
which those who think upon it regard as unseemly, and

consequently refuse to believe the resurrection of the flesh. But if a statue of some ductile metal were to be liquified by fire or crushed into powder or melted into a lump, and an artist had in mind to restore it again out of the same amount 15 of material, it would make no difference to the completeness of it which particle of the material were given back to which limb of the statue, provided that, when restored, it obtained back again that whole of which it had previously consisted. So also God, marvellously and ineffably an artist, will out of 20 that whole of which our flesh had consisted, reconstitute it with marvellous and ineffable celerity : and it will not affect its complete reconstruction whether hairs come back to hairs and nails to nails, or whether anything of these that was lost be converted into flesh and thus be brought back into other 25 parts of the body, so long as the Artist's providence takes care that nothing is made unseemly.

OF DIFFERENCES OF STATURE

90. Nor does it follow that because men have been tall or short when living, they will be tall or short when they live again, or that thin men will come to life again with the same thinness, or stout men with the same stoutness. But as it is in the Creator's counsels that, while in his own image there 5 is a conservation of each man's proper being and recognizable aspect, yet in respect of the rest of the body's possessions everything is reduced to equality, there will take place such a modification of that constituent material in each individual that, while nothing of it is lost, anything that any man is 10 short of will be supplied by him who has already shown his power to make out of nothing that which it has been his will to make. If, however, in the bodies of those who rise again there has to be some inequality which has reason for it, as there is inequality of the tones of which music is made, some- 15

thing will be done to each man in respect of the material
constituents of his own body which will both make the man
equal with the angel choirs and will present to their perceptions nothing that is incongruous. In fact no unseemly
20 thing will find a place there, but whatever there is will be
seemly, for its existence will only be justified on the ground
of its seemliness.

SPIRITUAL BODIES

91. Therefore the bodies of the saints will rise again free
from defect, free from deformity, free from any corruption
or burden or difficulty. In them facility will be matched
with felicity: which is why they are described as spiritual,[1]
5 though without controversy they will be bodies, and not
spirits. But as at this present it is described as an animate
body, while yet it is a body and not a soul, so at that time it
will be a spiritual body, while remaining a body, not a spirit.
Consequently as regards the corruption which now weighs
10 down the soul, and those defects by which the flesh lusts
against the spirit, it will then be no longer flesh, but body,
for we are told that there are celestial bodies.[2] That is the
explanation of *Flesh and blood shall not take possession of the
kingdom of God*: for, as though explaining his meaning, he
15 adds *Neither shall corruption take possession of incorruption.*[3]
The earlier expression "flesh and blood" is replaced
by "corruption", and "kingdom of God" by
"incorruption". Yet as regards its substance, it will still
be flesh: which is why, even after his resurrection, Christ's
20 body was referred to as flesh.[4] But the reason why the
apostle says, *It is sown an animate body; it will rise a spiritual
body*,[5] is that in those circumstances, when the spirit without

---

[1] Cf. 1 Cor. 15. 44.   [2] Cf. 1 Cor. 15. 40.
[3] 1 Cor. 15. 50.   [4] Cf. Luke 24. 39.   [5] 1 Cor. 15. 44.

the need of any intermediary vivifies the flesh subject to it, there will be such concord of flesh and spirit that we shall find no resistance from inside ourselves, but as we shall suffer 25 no enemy from without, neither shall we suffer ourselves as enemies within.

THE RESURRECTION TO CONDEMNATION

92. All, however, who are not released by the one Mediator of God and men from that mass of corruption which was caused by man at the first, will rise indeed no less than the others, each one along with his own flesh, but to be punished along with the devil and his angels. Whether 5 indeed these will rise with the defects and deformities of their own bodies, with any defective or deformed members they have had, there is no need for us to trouble to inquire. Nor ought we to worry ourselves about the aspect or appearance, which is uncertain, of people of whose ever- 10 lasting damnation we are certain. Nor should it concern us how in their case the body will be incorruptible while yet capable of pain, or how corruptible while incapable of dying. For there is no true life except where there is happy living, nor true incorruption except where health is cor- 15 rupted by no pain. Where, however, the unhappy is not permitted to die, death itself, so to speak, is deathless: and where continual pain afflicts without destroying, corruption itself is interminable. This is what Holy Scripture means by the second death.[1]
20

OF DEGREES OF ETERNAL PUNISHMENT

93. Yet neither the first death, by which the soul is compelled to leave its own body, nor the second, by which the

[1] Cf. Rev. 2. 11; 20. 14.

soul is not permitted to leave its penal body, would have
been man's lot if no man had sinned. Certainly the lightest
5 punishment of all will be theirs who, beyond the sin they
have contracted by origin, have added none besides: and
among the rest, who have made additions, each person will
find there his damnation the more tolerable the less the
iniquity he has shown while here.

BY CONTRAST THE SAINTS WILL THE BETTER APPRECIATE THE BENEFITS OF GOD'S GRACE

XXIV   94. Thus while the reprobate angels and men abide in
eternal punishment, then will the saints have deeper apprecia-
tion of the benefit which grace has bestowed upon them:
then by the facts themselves will be shown in greater evidence
5 the meaning of what is written in the psalm, *My song shall
be of mercy and judgement unto thee, O Lord*:[1] because except
by unmerited mercy no man is delivered, and except by
merited judgement no man is condemned.

OF PREDESTINATION AND ELECTION

95. Then will be revealed what now is hidden. When,
of two infants, one was to be taken by God's mercy, the
other to be left through his judgement, so that in him he that
was taken might be made aware of what was due to him by
5 judgement except that mercy came to the rescue, why was
the one taken rather than the other, when both were in the
same case?[2] Why were mighty works not done among
certain people, when, if they had been done, those men
would have repented, and why were they done among those
10 who were not going to believe? For our Lord says in clear

[1] Ps. 101. 1.
[2] Cf. Matt. 24. 41 with Mal. 1. 2, 3 and Rom. 9. 13.

language, *Woe unto thee, Chorazin! woe unto thee, Bethsaida!
for if the mighty works, which were done in you, had been done in
Tyre and Sidon, they would have repented long ago in sackcloth
and ashes.*[1]   Certainly not because it was God's unrighteous
will that they should not be saved, when they might have 15
been saved had he wished it.   Then will it appear in the
bright light of wisdom, what now the faith of the godly has
hold upon even before it appears in open recognition, how
sure and immutable and effective is the will of God; how
many things which he could do, it is not his will to do, yet 20
that nothing that he wills to do is beyond his power; and
how true that is which we sing in the psalm, *As for our God,
he is in heaven above: all things whatsoever he would, those hath
he done in heaven and in earth.*[2]   And this is not the truth if
there are things which he would, yet did not: and (what is 25
worse) if he failed to do them because the will of man
prevented the doing of what was the will of the Almighty.
Consequently, there is nothing done but that the will of the
Almighty is that it be done, either by permitting it to be done,
or else by doing it himself.   30

GOD'S ACT IS GOOD EVEN WHEN HE PERMITS EVIL

96. Nor is there room for doubt that God's act is good
even when he permits the doing of things that are evil.   For
this permission is given by nothing else but righteous judgement, and evidently everything that is righteous is a good
thing.   Consequently, although things which are evil, in so 5
far as they are evil, are not good, yet that there should exist
not only good things, but also evil things, is a good thing.
For unless it were a good thing that evil things too should
exist, their existence would in no wise be permitted by one
both good and almighty: for evidently such a one finds it 10

[1] Matt. 11. 21.   [2] Ps. 115. 3.

as easy not to permit that which is against his will, as to perform what is his will. Unless this is our conviction, the first sentence of our Creed is in peril: for in it we profess that we believe in God the Father Almighty. For the word
15 "Almighty", if used truthfully, can only mean that he has power to do whatever it is his will to do, and that the will of the Almighty is not hindered of its effectiveness by the will of any creature whatsoever.

"WILL HAVE ALL MEN TO BE SAVED"

97. Therefore we need to inquire in what sense the statement was made that God *will have all men to be saved*: [1] for in this case too the apostle has spoken with absolute truth. For since not all are being saved—indeed by far the greater
5 number are not—it appears as if that which God wishes to take place is not doing so, because (as it seems) human will is impeding the will of God. For when we ask for the reason why not all are being saved, the answer usually given is "Because they themselves will not have it so". But this
10 cannot be true of infants, who are as yet incapable of either assent or refusal. For should we decide that we ought to impute to their will the childish movements they make when they are baptized, resisting as much as their powers permit, we should affirm that they are saved even against their will.
15 Clearer still are the words spoken by our Lord in the Gospel in his apostrophe to the godless city, *How often would I have gathered thy sons together, as a hen her chickens, and thou wouldest not*: [2] as though the will of God had been overborne by the will of men, and through the hindrance of those weak ones
20 that would not, the Most Mighty had been unable to accomplish what he would. And what has become of that omnipotence by which he has done whatever things he would

[1] I Tim. 2. 4.   [2] Matt. 23. 37.

both in heaven and in earth, if it was his will to gather the
sons of Jerusalem, yet he failed to do so? Or was it perhaps
that Jerusalem refused to have her sons gathered by him? 25
Hardly: for even against her will he did gather such of her
sons as he would; because the statement is, not that some
things he would do and did do, while other things he would
do and did not do, but *all things whatsoever he would, those
hath he done in heaven and in earth.* 30

ST PAUL'S DOCTRINE OF GOD'S GRACE IN PREDESTINATION

98. Who then is so profanely foolish as to affirm that God XXV
is unable to turn to a good effect the evil wills of men, those
which he would, when he would, where he would? But
when he does this, it is through mercy that he does it: when
he does not do it, it is through judgement that he does not: 5
*for he hath mercy upon whom he will, and whom he will he
hardeneth.*[1] The apostle's purpose in saying this was the
commendation of grace: for it was in commendation of
grace that he had already made reference to those twins in
Rebecca's womb, that *when these were not yet born, nor had done* 10
*anything good or evil, that the purpose of God according to election
might stand, not of works but of him that calleth, it was said to her,
The elder shall serve the younger.*[2] And to the same effect he
adduced a further prophetic testimony, where it is written,
Jacob have I loved, but Esau have I hated.[3] But perceiving how 15
the statement thus made was capable of distressing those who
were incapable of penetrating with their intelligence into
such a depth of grace, he proceeds, *What shall we say then?
Is there unrighteousness with God? God forbid.*[4] For it has
the appearance of unrighteousness, that apart from any merits 20

[1] Rom. 9. 18.　　　　[2] Rom. 9. 11, 12; Gen. 25. 23.
[3] Rom. 9. 13; Mal. 1. 2, 3.　　　[4] Rom. 9. 14.

of good or evil works God should love the one and hate the
other. And incidentally, if he had wished us to understand
the future good works of the one or evil works of the
other, works which of course God had in his foreknowledge,
25 he would certainly not have said "not of works" but
"of works which were to be": in that way he would
have answered our present question, or rather, would have
presented no question which needed answering. As it is,
however, having answered *God forbid*, meaning " God forbid
30 that there should be unrighteousness with God ", he immediately adds, by way of proof that this is done without
unrighteousness on God's part, *For he saith unto Moses, I will
have mercy upon whom I will have mercy, and I will have compassion upon whom I will have compassion*.[1] For who but a
35 fool will think God unrighteous, whether he visits penal
judgement upon one who deserves it or affords mercy to one
who deserves it not? Finally the apostle draws his
conclusion, saying, *So then it is not of him that willeth, nor of
him that runneth, but of God that hath mercy*.[2] It appears then
40 that both the twins were born by nature sons of wrath, not
indeed through any works of their own, but by origin from
Adam bound in the chain of damnation. But God who said,
I will have mercy upon whom I will have mercy, loved Jacob
through compassion undeserved, but hated Esau through
45 judgement that was due. And since this judgement was
due to both of them, the one had cause to see in the other
that there was no matter for glorying in any distinguishing
merits of his own, in that, though in the same case, he did
not incur the same chastisement, but rather for glorying in
50 the generosity of divine grace, in that it is *not of him that
willeth, nor of him that runneth, but of God that hath mercy*. In
fact, in a most profound and salutary mystery, the whole aspect
and (so to speak) countenance of the Holy Scriptures is found

[1] Rom. 9. 15; Ex. 33. 19. [2] Rom. 9. 16.

to give this admonition to those who look well upon it, that
he that glorieth should glory in the Lord.[1]   55

THE SAME, CONTINUED

99. Having then commended God's mercy in the state-
ment, *So then it is not of him that willeth, nor of him that runneth,
but of God that hath mercy,*[2] his next intention was to commend God's judgement, in that, upon whom mercy is not
shown, no unrighteousness is done, but judgement, seeing there 5
is no unrighteousness with God : so he immediately proceeds
to add, *For the scripture saith unto Pharaoh, For this cause have
I raised thee up, that I may display my power in thee, and that my
name may be declared throughout all the earth.*[3] After this
quotation he sums up both themes, both mercy and judge- 10
ment, in the words *So then* God *hath mercy upon whom he
will, and whom he will he hardeneth* : [4] " hath mercy ", that is,
by his great goodness, " hardeneth ", not by any unrighteousness : with the result that he that is set free may not glory of
his own deserts, nor he that is condemned make complaint 15
except of his own deserts.   For it is grace alone that separates
the redeemed from the lost : for a cause common to both,
a cause derived from their origin, had compacted them both
into one mass of perdition.   But if any man, on hearing this,
is so misguided as to say, *Why doth he yet find fault ? for who* 20
doth resist his will ?,[5] hinting that the evil man should not be
held to blame, seeing that God has mercy upon whom he
will, and whom he will he hardens, let us by no means be
ashamed to give the same answer as we perceive the apostle
gave : *O man, who art thou that repliest against God ? Doth* 25
*the thing formed say unto him that formed it, Why hast thou made
me thus ? Or hath not the potter power over the clay, out of the*

[1] Cf. 1 Cor. 1. 31.   [2] Rom. 9. 16.   [3] Rom. 9. 17; Ex. 9. 16.
[4] Rom. 9. 18.   [5] Rom. 9. 19.

H

same lump to make one vessel unto honour, and another unto dis-
honour ? [1] At this point certain foolish persons suppose that
30 the apostle was at a loss what to answer, and, for lack of a
reason worth giving, rebuked the boldness of the gainsayer.
But there is great weight in the observation, *O man, who art*
thou ? In questions of this kind it recalls a man to the
consideration of his own capacities. It is a brief expression;
35 yet in reality it renders a very sound reason. For if a man
does not comprehend these things, who is he, that he should
reply against God? If he does comprehend them, he is the
less inventive in finding anything to reply. For if he does comprehend, he perceives that the whole human race was, in its
40 apostate origin, condemned with so righteous a judgement
of God that even if no man were delivered from that judgement, none would have the right to complain of God's
righteousness: and that those who are delivered were of
necessity so delivered that by the majority who were not
45 delivered, but were left in most righteous condemnation, it
might be shown what were the deserts of the whole leavening,
as well as where the merited judgement of God would have
led even them except that his unmerited mercy came to their
rescue: that thus every mouth of such as would glory in
50 their own merits should be stopped, and that he that glorieth
should glory in the Lord.[2]

OF ACTS DONE CONTRARY TO GOD'S WILL, YET
NOT IN SPITE OF HIS WILL

XXVI   100. These are the *great works of the Lord, sought out unto*
all his good wills,[3] sought out with such wisdom that when
angelic and human creatures had sinned (that is, had done
not his will but their own) he himself fulfilled what was his

---

[1] Rom. 9. 20, 21.   [2] Cf. 1 Cor. 1. 31.
[3] LXX Ps. 110. 2 (111. 2).

own will, and did so by making use of that same will of 5
created beings by which that had been done which was
contrary to the Creator's will: for, in his supreme goodness,
he made good use even of the evil, for the condemnation of
those whom he righteously predestinated to punishment,
and for the salvation of those whom of his kindness he pre- 10
destinated to grace. For, as far as they themselves are
concerned, they acted contrary to God's will: but, as concerns
God's omnipotence, they had no power at all to accomplish
their act. For by the very fact that they acted contrary to
his will, his will was made effective upon them. For the 15
truth of the statement that *the works of the Lord are great,
sought out unto all his good wills*, consists pre-eminently in this,
that in a marvellous and ineffable manner even what is done
contrary to his will, is not done in spite of his will: for it
would not be done unless he permitted it, and his permission 20
is not unwilling but willing: nor, being good, would he
permit an evil act, if he were not by his omnipotence able
even of the evil to make a good effect.

A MAN'S GOOD WILL SOMETIMES DOES NOT
COINCIDE WITH GOD'S WILL

101. There are, however, occasions when a man, with a
good will, wills something which God does not will, while
God's will also is much more abundantly and much more
assuredly good—for God's will can never in any case be evil:
for example, when a good son will have his father to live, 5
whereas God, by his good will, will have him to die. And
the opposite can happen, that a man should will the same
by an evil will as God wills with his good will: as when a
bad son will have his father to die, and this is God's will also.
The former, in short, wishes for what is not God's will, while 10
the latter wishes for what is God's will: and yet the filial

affection of the former is more consonant with the good will of God, though his object is at variance, than is the dis-affection of the latter in spite of his object being the same. 15 It makes a great difference therefore, in the assignment of approval or disapproval, what it is competent for a man to will, and what for God to will, as well as towards what end this man or that directs his will. For God fulfils some of the things he wills, which of course are good, by means of the 20 evil wills of evil men : for example, it was by the Jews whose will was evil that by the good will of the Father Christ was slain for us : and this was a good of such magnitude that when the apostle Peter expressed his will for it not to be so, he was addressed as Satan by the very one who had come to be 25 slain.[1] Or consider how good in appearance was the will of the affectionate faithful who were unwilling for the apostle Paul to go to Jerusalem, lest he should there suffer the things the prophet Agabus had foretold : [2] and yet it was God's will that he should suffer these things for the publishing of the 30 faith of Christ : it was as a martyr of Christ that God was training him. And that good will of his he did not bring to fulfilment by the good wills of the Christians but by the evil wills of the Jews : yet those were more closely in agreement with him whose will was at variance with his, than were 35 those by whose willing act his will was actually done : because though these men's object was the same, God acted through them by his good will, whereas they acted by a will that was evil.

GOD'S WILL ALWAYS PREVAILS

102. Yet however strong may be the wills, whether of angels or of men, whether these be good or evil, whether the object of those wills be the same as God's or other than God's,

[1] Cf. Matt. 16. 22, 23.   [2] Cf. Acts 21. 12.

the will of God, who is almighty, is always invincible: and
it can under no circumstances be an evil will, since even when 5
it visits with evil it is righteous, and inevitably, being
righteous, it is not evil. Therefore God the Almighty,
whether through his compassion he has mercy upon whom
he will, or through his judgement he hardens whom he will,
neither does anything unrighteously nor does anything at all 10
unless he wills it, but all things that he wills he brings to
effect.

" WILL HAVE ALL MEN TO BE SAVED "

103. And consequently when we hear it said, and read it XXVII
in Holy Scripture, that he will have all men to be saved,
although it is abundantly clear to us that not all men are being
saved, we ought not on that account to attribute any limita-
tions to God's most almighty will. Rather we ought to 5
understand the text, *Who will have all men to be saved*,[1] as
though what it said was that no man obtains salvation except
such as it has been his will should be saved—not that no man
exists except such as it is his will should be saved, but that
none does obtain salvation except whom he will, and that 10
therefore request should be made to him that it may be his
will, because if it is his will, the man's salvation of necessity
follows. In fact when the apostle made this statement, he
was concerned with prayer to God. In the same way we
interpret what is written in the Gospel, *Who lighteth every* 15
man [2]—not that there exists no man who is not enlightened,
but that no man is enlightened except by him. Or in any
case in *Who will have all men to be saved* the meaning is not
as though there were no man whom he would not have to be
saved, for he did in fact refuse to do mighty works and 20
miracles among people who he says would have repented if

[1] 1 Tim. 2. 4.   [2] John 1. 9.

he had done them: but that we should understand by "all
men" the whole human race, as differentiated into all sorts
and kinds, kings and commoners, noble and ignoble, high
25 and low, learned and unlearned, whole in body or weakly,
quick-minded or slow or fools, rich or poor or of moderate
means, men and women and babes and children, growing
boys and girls, the young, the middle-aged, the elderly: of
all tongues, of all manners and customs, of all crafts, of all
30 professions, of all the innumerable variety of wills and
consciences, and whatever else there is that makes for
differentiation among men. Is there any of these classes
from which it is not God's will that throughout all nations
men should be saved through his only-begotten Son our Lord?
35 And as it is his will, he also performs it, seeing the Almighty
cannot will in vain whatever he has made his will. The
apostle had already given the injunction that prayer should be
made for all men, and had added in particular, *For kings and
those that are in high estate*: for such might be supposed,
40 through arrogance and worldly pride, to be out of sympathy
with the humility of Christian faith. After that he says,
For this is good in the sight of God our Saviour, meaning that
prayer should be made even for such as these: and then, to
leave no room for despairing, he added, *Who will have all
45 men to be saved and come into the knowledge of the truth.*[1] This
in fact is what God has judged a good thing, that through the
prayers of the humble he should vouchsafe to afford salvation
to the proud: and this we see has already actually been
accomplished. Our Lord also made use of this figure of
50 speech in the Gospel when he said to the Pharisees, *Ye tithe
mint and rue and every herb.*[2] For it is not true that the
Pharisees tithed all the herbs, including those in other
countries and those belonging to foreigners in every land. As
then here we understand "every herb" to mean every kind

---

[1] 1 Tim. 2. 1-4.   [2] Luke 11. 42.

of herb, so in the other place we can understand " all men " 55
to mean every kind of men.   Or it can be understood in any
other way whatever, so long as we are not induced to think
that it was the will of the almighty God that something
should be done and it has not been done : for without any
sort of doubt, if (as the truth of the psalm has it) he has 60
done all things that he would both in heaven and in earth,
certainly whatever it is he has not done, that it was not his
will to do.

OF GOD'S FOREKNOWLEDGE OF ADAM'S SIN

104. From this it follows that if God had foreknown that XXVIII
the first man would have the permanent will to continue
without sin as he had been made, it would have been his
will also to preserve him in that salvation in which he was
created, and in due time, after the birth of children, to promote 5
him, without the interposition of death, to a better state in
which he would have been incapable not only of committing
sin but even of having the will to sin.   But because he fore-
knew that the man would make ill use of his free choice, and
thus commit sin, he preferred rather to prepare his own will 10
beforehand for such a contingency, so as himself to do good
even with one that was doing ill, that thus the good will of
the Almighty might not be stultified by the evil will of man,
but might be fulfilled none the less on account of it.

OF PRIMARY AND ULTIMATE FREEDOM OF CHOICE

105. For it was right and proper that man should first be
created in this state of being capable of either good will or
evil, and neither be unrewarded if it were good nor un-
punished if it were evil.   But afterwards he will be in the
state of being incapable of an evil will, but will not on that 5

account have been deprived of his free choice. In fact that choice will be much more free which will be entirely incapable of serving sin. For there is no cause to complain of that will, nor does it cease to be a will or to be rightly 10 designated free, by which our will towards blessedness is of such a character that we not only have not the will towards wretchedness but are altogether incapable of having it. As then even in this life our soul has the will to refuse unhappiness, so it will for ever have the will to refuse iniquity. 15 But there was no means of forgoing the proper order in which it was God's will to make it evident how good a creature is the rational animate being, which has the capacity even of not sinning, though that is better which has not the capacity of sinning: as likewise that was a lesser immortality, yet it 20 was an immortality, in which he was capable even of not dying, though that immortality will be a greater in which he will not be capable of dying.

MAN HAS NO DESERTS APART FROM GOD'S GRACE

106. That former immortality human nature has lost through its free choice : the latter it will receive as a gift through grace, though if it had not sinned, the intention was that it should receive it through its deserts. And yet, even 5 so, there could have been no deserts apart from grace. For even though sin stood in free choice and nothing else, free choice itself did not suffice for the conservation of righteousness, unless by participation in the immutable goodness it were furnished with divine aid. For as it is in a man's power 10 to die when he will (for any man can make an end of himself, to mention no other means, at least by refusing his food) yet his will alone is not sufficient for the retention of life in the absence of the aids either of food or of any other safeguards there may be : so man in paradise was competent by his will

alone to make an end of himself by apostasy from righteous- 15
ness, yet for his retention of the life of righteousness his will
was not sufficient apart from the aid of God who had made
him. But, since the time of that collapse, God's compassion
is the greater : for now even choice itself has to be set free
from servitude, since sin along with death has dominion over 20
it. And it is being set free, not in any respect by its own
efforts, but solely by the grace of God which is set in the
faith of Christ, and that in such a manner that (as it is written)
the will itself is prepared beforehand by the Lord [1] so that by
it there may be an acceptance of the rest of those gifts of God 25
by which men come to the gift eternal.

GOD'S WILL MUST BE DONE, EITHER BY MAN
OR UPON MAN

107. This is why even eternal life, though certainly the
reward of good works, is by the apostle characterized as
God's grace : *For*, he says, *the wages of sin is death, but the
grace of God is eternal life in Christ Jesus our Lord.*[2] Wages for
military service is a debt that is paid, not a gift that is given : 5
and so he says, *The wages of sin is death*, pointing out that
death is visited upon sin not as something undeserved but as a
thing due. Grace, however, unless it is given gratis, is not
grace. We must understand then that even the good deserts
of a man are God's gifts : and when these receive the reward 10
of eternal life, what is this but the return of grace for grace ? [3]
Consequently, man was in such sense created upright [4] that
while he was incapable of abiding in that uprightness apart
from divine aid, yet he could become crooked by his own
choice. Whichever of these he should choose, the will of 15
God would be done, either perhaps by the man, or at least

---

[1] Cf. LXX Prov. 8. 35.   [2] Rom. 6. 23.
[3] John 1. 16.   [4] Cf. Eccles. 7. 29.

upon him. At length, because he preferred to do his own
will and not God's, the will of God was done upon him : for
out of one and the same mass of perdition which has
20 proceeded from the man's offspring, God makes one vessel
to honour and another to dishonour [1]—to honour by
compassion, to dishonour by judgement—that no one
should glory in man, and (by the same token) no man should
glory in himself.

IF CHRIST WERE NOT GOD, HE COULD NOT BE A MEDIATOR

108. For not even by the one Mediator of God and man,
the Man Christ Jesus, could our deliverance be accomplished
if he were not also God. Now when Adam was created,
created man and created upright, there was no need of a
5 mediator : when, however, the human race had by its sins
been removed very far from God, we had need to be
reconciled to God. And this must needs be done by the
Mediator who alone was sinlessly born and lived and was put
to death : and it must result in the resurrection of the flesh
10 unto life eternal. Thus by means of God's humility would
man's pride be both rebuked and healed : by the fact of his
being called back to God through God become incarnate,
man would be brought to see how far removed he had gone
from God : through the Man who is God an example of
15 obedience would be set before man's obstinacy : while the
Only-begotten took the form of a servant, a form which had
no previous merits of its own, a fount of grace would be laid
open, as also the resurrection of the flesh, which was promised
to the redeemed, would be exemplified beforehand in none
20 other than the Redeemer : and by that same human nature
which he rejoiced at having seduced, the devil would be

[1] Cf. Rom. 9. 21.

vanquished, yet man would not therefore glory, lest pride
should a second time be born : to which we may add whatever else the more proficient may perceive and express in
words regarding this great mystery of the Mediator—or 25
perhaps only perceive, but not express.

BETWEEN DEATH AND RESURRECTION

109. But during the time which intervenes between a XXIX
man's death and the resurrection at the last, men's souls are
reserved in secret storehouses, at rest or in tribulation
according to each soul's deserts, according to its lot in the
flesh during life.   5

OF OFFERINGS AND ALMS FOR THE DEPARTED

110. Nor is there room for denial that the souls of the
deceased obtain relief through the dutiful service of their
friends who are alive, when the Mediator's sacrifice is offered
for them or almsgiving is done in the Church. Such acts,
however, are of advantage to those who during their life 5
have deserved that such acts should be of advantage to them.
For there is a certain manner of living, neither good enough
to dispense with the need for these after death, nor bad
enough to preclude their being of advantage to it after death ;
and there is a manner of living which is so established in 10
goodness as to dispense with the need for them, as again there
is one so established in evil as to be incapable of benefiting
even from these when it has passed on from this life. Therefore it is here and now that a man acquires any merit or
demerit through which after this life he becomes capable of 15
relief or depression. So let no man expect that after his
death he can make up in the sight of God for his omissions
while here. Thus these services which the Church repeatedly

performs for the commendation of the departed are in no
20 sense opposed to that apostolic statement which says: *For
we shall all stand before the judgement-seat of Christ, that each
one may receive in accordance with the things he has done in the
body, whether it be good or bad:* [1] because each of them, while
living in the body, has acquired for himself even this merit,
25 the possibility of their being of advantage to him. For they
are not of advantage to everybody. And why are they not
of advantage to everybody, unless because of the difference
between the life which each one has lived in the body? At
such times then as the sacrifices either of the altar or of any
30 manner of alms are offered for all the baptized departed, on
behalf of the very good they are thanksgivings, on behalf of
the not very bad they are propitiations, while on behalf of
the very bad, though they are no sort of assistance to the
dead, they are some sort of consolation to the living. And
35 in cases where they are of advantage, the advantage is either
that they obtain complete remission, or at least that damnation itself becomes less intolerable.

OF THE TWO CITIES, ONE OF CHRIST, THE OTHER
OF THE DEVIL

III. After the resurrection, however, when the universal
judgement is finished and complete, those two cities will
each have its own bounds: one is Christ's, the other the
devil's: one will consist of the good, the other of the wicked:
5 and each of them will contain both angels and men. The
good will no longer have any will for sinning; the wicked
will no longer have the power: nor will either of them have
it in them to die, since those will live in truth and felicity in
life eternal, while these will continue to exist in infelicity in
10 eternal death without any possibility of dying, and in both

[1] Rom. 14. 10; 2 Cor. 5. 10.

cases without any end. The former will abide in beatitude, though not all of equal dignity; the latter will abide in misery, which not all will find equally insupportable.

OF ETERNAL PUNISHMENT

112. It is then without good reason that some, or rather, a great many, do through their human affections think with pity upon the eternal punishment of the damned and their perpetual and unintermitted torments, and refuse to believe it will be so: not indeed that they set themselves in opposition 5 to divine Scripture, but that in accordance with their own feelings they tone down all its hard sayings, and twist to a gentler verdict things in Scripture which they suppose were spoken more for the sake of inspiring terror than of stating the truth. "For", say they, "*God will not forget to have* 10 *mercy, nor will he in his wrath shut up his loving-kindnesses.*" [1] Certainly we read it so in the holy psalm. But, without any doubt, it is to be understood of those who are designated *vessels of mercy*: [2] for these also are delivered from misery not for any merits of theirs, but through the mercy of God. 15 Even if they think this text applies to all men, it does not follow that they must suppose there can be an end to the damnation of those referred to in the saying, *And these shall go into eternal punishment*: for if so, one would need to surmise that there will some time be an end also of the felicity of 20 those referred to in the contrary statement, *But the righteous into eternal life.*[3] But there is no harm in their thinking, if this gives them pleasure, that the penalties of the damned are at certain intervals of time somewhat eased. For the statement that the wrath of God abides upon them [4] (and by 25 "the wrath of God" we mean neither more nor less than

---

[1] Ps. 77. 9.　　　　　　　　[2] Rom. 9. 23.
[3] Matt. 25. 46.　　　　　　　[4] John 3. 36.

damnation : for this is the meaning of " wrath of God ", not
some perturbation of the divine mind) can be understood in
the sense that " in his wrath ", that is, while his wrath is
30 ever-abiding, yet he " shuts not up his loving-kindnesses ",
not because he sets a time-limit to eternal punishment, but
because he affords some ease or intermission to their torments :
for even the psalm does not say " so as to bring his wrath to
an end ", or " when his wrath is ended ", but " in his wrath ".
35 And if this wrath by itself were the very slightest that in such
circumstances can be imagined—to perish from the kingdom
of God, to be driven out from the city of God, to be alienated
from the life of God, to be deprived of that great abundance
of God's sweetness which he has laid up for them that fear
40 him but has accomplished for them that hope in him [1]—
so great is this punishment, that no torments we have
experience of can be compared to it : for it is eternal, whereas
these, however many ages they persist, are no more than
lengthy.

EVERLASTING DEATH, AND ETERNAL LIFE

113. So then that everlasting death of the damned, that is,
their alienation from the life of God,[2] will be permanent and
without end, and it will be common to them all without
exception, whatever guesses men may make, under the
5 influence of their own human affections, with regard to
variation in the punishments, or the easing or the intermission
of pain : and likewise the eternal life of the saints will have a
permanency common to them all, whatever differences of
dignity there may be in their concordant glory.

[1] Cf. Ps. 31. 19.   [2] Cf. Eph. 4. 18.

CONCERNING HOPE, AND THE NEED FOR PRAYER

114. This confession of the faith, briefly comprised in the XXX
Creed, when carnally regarded is milk for babes, but
spiritually considered and expounded is food for strong men:
and of it is born the good hope of the faithful, with holy
charity as its attendant. But from among all the matters 5
which are the object of faith and belief, those and no others
have reference to hope which are comprised in the Lord's
Prayer. For, as the divine oracles testify, *Cursed is every man
that putteth his hope in a man*: [1] and consequently any man
who puts his hope in himself is involved in the meshes of this 10
curse. For which reason we ought to ask of the Lord God,
and of him alone, whatever it is we hope either to perform of
good works or to receive as the reward of good works
accomplished.

THE LORD'S PRAYER IN ST MATTHEW

115. Hence it appears in the evangelist Matthew that the
Lord's Prayer comprises seven petitions, and in three of these
requests are made for eternal things, in the other four for
things temporal, yet such as are necessary with a view to
obtaining things eternal. For the things we pray for in the 5
clauses, *Hallowed be thy name: Thy kingdom come: Thy
will be done, as in heaven, so in earth* [2] (which some have quite
reasonably interpreted "in the spirit and in the body"), must
most certainly be kept hold of for ever. They have their
beginning here and now, and the more we progress the more 10
they are increased in us: but when made perfect, which is
what we must hope for in another life, they will become our
permanent possession. But the clauses, *Give us this day our
daily bread: And forgive us our debts, as we also forgive our*

[1] Jer. 17. 5.   [2] Matt. 6. 9, 10.

15 *debtors: And bring us not into temptation: But deliver us from*
evil [1]—these quite obviously apply to the needs of our present
life. So then in that eternal life in which we hope we shall
abide for ever, both the hallowing of God's name, and his
kingdom, and his will, will in our spirit and body be
20 permanent and perfect and immortal. But the bread is
referred to as " daily bread " because of our present need for
so much of it as soul and flesh require, whether we understand
the word " bread " in a spiritual or in a carnal sense or in
both. Also the forgiveness we ask for belongs to this present,
25 in which there is commission of sins : in this present are the
temptations which either entice us or urge us to sin : in this
present, in fact, is the evil from which we desire to be
delivered. In that other place there is none of these.

THE LORD'S PRAYER IN ST LUKE

116. But the evangelist Luke includes in the Lord's Prayer
not seven petitions but five : [2] yet he is not in disagreement
with Matthew, but by his very brevity indicates how those
seven are to be interpreted. The hallowing of God's name
5 takes place in the spirit, whereas God's kingdom is to come
at the resurrection of the flesh. Luke therefore, wishing to
show that the third petition is in some sort a repetition of the
previous two, has made its meaning more clear by omitting
it. Next he sets down three more, relating to daily bread,
10 the forgiveness of sins, and the avoidance of temptation. But
the one Matthew places at the end, *But deliver us from evil,*
Luke has left out, so that we should understand that it
attaches to the previous one which refers to temptation.
That is why it says " But deliver ", not " And deliver ", as if
15 making it clear that there is one petition, " Not this but

---

[1] Matt. 6. 11–13.   [2] Luke 11. 2 ff.

that ", so that any man may see that his deliverance from evil consists of his not being brought into temptation.

117. Now as regards charity, the apostle has pronounced XXXI it greater than those other two, faith and hope:[1] and the more of it there is in any man, the better the character of the man in whom it is. For when the question is raised whether so-and-so is a good man, we are not asking what he believes 5 or what he hopes for, but how much he loves. For a man who loves as he ought, unquestionably believes and hopes as he ought: whereas he who does not love believes in vain,[2] even though the objects of his belief be true, and also hopes in vain, even though the objects of his hope be shown to have 10 reference to the true felicity: for his faith and his hope must have at least this content, that in answer to his prayer there can be granted him the grace to love. For although hope without love is impossible, it is conceivable that he may fail to love that which is essential to the attainment of his hope: 15 for example, one might hope for life eternal (and to whom is this not an object of love?), yet not love righteousness, without which no man attains to eternal life. This is that faith of Christ which the apostle speaks so well of, the faith which worketh by affection:[3] and whatever it may be that 20 this faith does not yet have in its affection, it asks so that it may receive it, seeks so that it may find it, and knocks so that the door may be opened to it.[4] Now faith obtains on demand what the law puts forth as a command. For apart from the gift of God, that is, apart from the Holy Spirit by whom 25 charity is poured forth in our hearts,[5] the law can command but not commend, nay more, may even make into a trans-

---

[1] I Cor. 13. 13.   [2] Cf. I Cor. 15. 2, 17.
[3] Gal. 5. 6.   [4] Matt. 7. 7.   [5] Cf. Rom. 5. 5.

I

gressor one whom it deprives of the excuse of ignorance.
For where there is no divine charity, there is the reign of
30 carnal cupidity.

THE FOUR STAGES OF MAN'S PROGRESS

118. Now man's first estate is to live according to the flesh
in the profound darkness of ignorance, and without any
opposition from reason. Next, when by the law there has
come the knowledge of sin,[1] man, if not yet assisted by the
5 divine Spirit, while desiring to live according to the law,
finds himself overcome: he sins with full knowledge, and
becomes the subject and servant of sin (*For of whom a man is
overcome, to the same is he also subjected as a bondservant*[2]): for
the knowledge of the commandment has the effect that sin
10 works in the man all manner of concupiscence,[3] transgression
reaches its climax, and thus the Scripture is fulfilled that
The law entered in besides, so that the offence might abound.[4]
Such is man's second estate. But if God has looked upon
him, and is believed to give his personal help towards the
15 fulfilment of his commandments, and man begins to be led
by the Spirit of God,[5] there ensues a lust against the flesh
under the stronger power of charity; and thus, although man
still experiences resistance from within himself so long as the
whole of his sickness is not healed, yet as an outcome of faith
20 the righteous man lives,[6] and lives righteously, in so far as
he does not surrender to evil concupiscence, but the delights
of righteousness obtain the victory. This is the third estate
of the man of good hope: and if in it a man makes progress
by pious perseverance, there remains that final peace which
25 after this life will have its fulfilment, first in the repose of the
spirit and afterwards also in the resurrection of the flesh.

---

[1] Cf. Rom. 3. 20.   [2] 2 Pet. 2. 19.   [3] Cf. Rom. 7. 8.
[4] Rom. 5. 20.   [5] Cf. Rom. 8. 14.   [6] Cf. Rom. 1. 17.

Of these four divisions the first is anterior to the law, the second under the law, the third under grace, and the fourth in full and perfect peace. Such has been the progressive development of the people of God through the course of time : 30 for such was God's pleasure, who ordereth all things in measure and number and weight.[1] For primarily it was anterior to law : secondly, under the law which was given by Moses : and next, under the grace which was revealed through the first advent of the Mediator. Yet this grace was not 35 lacking even aforetime to those to whom it was suitable for it to be imparted : though through the circumstances of that time it was veiled and hidden. For not one of the ancient righteous men had power to find salvation apart from the faith of Christ : nor, for that matter, if he had not been 40 known even to them, could he, at some times more openly, at others more obscurely, have been prophesied to us by their ministry.

THE GRACE OF REGENERATION CONVEYS COMPLETE REMISSION

119. But in whichsoever of these four periods (if that term be allowed) the grace of regeneration comes upon each individual person, in it he obtains remission of all his previous sins without exception, at the same time as that guilt which he contracted at birth is cancelled by his new birth : and so true 5 it is that *The Spirit bloweth where he listeth*,[2] that some persons, escaping any experience of that second stage of servitude under the law, begin to receive divine aid at the same time as they become aware of the commandment.

[1] Wisd. 11. 20. [2] Cf. John 3. 8.

AN EARLY DEATH WILL NOT DEPRIVE THE
REGENERATE OF ETERNAL LIFE

XXXII　120. For all that, a man cannot become capable of receiving
the commandment until after he has lived according to the
flesh.　Yet if he is at this point washed with the sacrament of
regeneration, death will be no harm to him if at that stage
5 he departs out of this life: for to this purpose has Christ both
died and risen again, that he may be Lord both of the living
and of the dead,[1] and the kingdom of death will have no hold
upon one for whom he has died who is free among the
dead.[2]

CHARITY IS THE END OF ALL THE COMMANDMENTS

121. So then all the divine precepts are referred back to
charity, of which the apostle says, *But the end of the precept
is charity out of a pure heart and of a good conscience and of faith
unfeigned.*[3]　Thus the end of every precept is charity: that
5 is, to charity every precept is referred back.　Any act, however, which is done either for fear of punishment or with
some carnal intention, in such sort as not to be referred back
to that charity which the Holy Spirit pours forth in our
hearts, is not as yet being done as it ought to be done, how-
10 ever much it seems to be.　This charity is towards God and
towards one's neighbour, and of course on these two precepts
hangs the whole Law, and the Prophets:[4] and you can add,
the Gospel and the Apostles.　For the statement, *The end of
the precept is charity*, is from the same source as *God is charity*.[5]
15 All things then which God commands (one of which is,
Thou shalt not commit adultery [6]) and all which are not a

---

[1] Cf. Rom. 14. 9.　　　　[2] Cf. Ps. 88. 5.
[3] 1 Tim. 1. 5.　　　　　[4] Cf. Matt. 22. 40.
[5] Rom. 13. 10; 1 John 4. 16.　　[6] Rom. 13. 9.

matter of command but of advice given in a special case (one
of which is, *It is good for a man not to touch a woman* [1]) are
rightly performed when they are referred back to our loving
God, and our neighbour for God's sake, both in this world 20
and in the world to come—our loving God now by faith,
but then by sight, and our neighbour too now by faith.   For
as mortals we have no knowledge of mortal men's hearts.
But in that world God will throw light upon the hidden
things of darkness and will make manifest the thoughts of 25
the heart, and then shall each man have praise from God: [2]
because each man will be able to praise and to love in his
neighbour precisely that upon which, to prevent it from
escaping notice, light will be thrown by none other than
God. Also cupidity decreases as charity increases, until 30
charity attain to such magnitude as cannot be surpassed.   For
*greater charity hath no man, than that a man lay down his life for
his friends.* [3]   And can any explain how great that charity
will be where there remains no cupidity for it even to check
and overcome?   For there will be health most perfect, when 35
there is no contention from death. [4]

CONCLUSION OF THIS WORK

122. So let us at length bring this volume to an end.   You XXXIII
yourself can decide whether you need call it a manual or keep
it for one.   For my part I thought your zeal in Christ ought
not to be discouraged, since I both believe and hope for good
things concerning you by the aid of our Redeemer, and have 5
the highest affection for you among his members.   So I have
written you this book, and have put my best into it.   I would
it were as serviceable as it is lengthy.   Its title is " Concerning
Faith, Hope, and Charity ".

[1] 1 Cor. 7. 1.   [2] Cf. 1 Cor. 4. 5.
[3] John 15. 13.   [4] Cf. Lat. 1 Cor. 15. 55.

NOTES

CHAPTER 3

2 charity. There are in this work three Latin substantives signifying "love". They are *caritas, dilectio, amor*: in the present translation, for purposes of clarity, they are represented respectively by "charity", "affection", "love": though in many places "love" would be more in accordance with modern English usage. *Amor* is as a rule used by St Augustine of human love (§ 68): but see also § 8. *Dilectio* is the expression or outward manifestation of the *caritas* which is at the foundation of the Christian character. *Caritas* in classical Latin meant "dearness", either of price or of personal esteem, but in Christian usage it had become the equivalent of the Greek *ăgăpē*. This word seems to have been invented by the Greek translators of the Old Testament, perhaps by assonance with the Hebrew *ahaba* and by analogy with the Greek verb *ăgăpō* (which means "I am content with"). There are in Greek several words which mean "love" of various kinds, but none of them was suitable to describe this new experience, within revealed religion, of the love of God and of man's response to it. Hence a new word was called for. The two verbs *amare* and *diligere* are used throughout this book apparently without any very significant difference of meaning: though, if one examines the matter carefully, *amo* will appear to mean, I love someone (or something) for my sake, *diligo* I love him for his sake.

CHAPTER 7

1 the Creed, *symbolum.* The contents of the Creed are in this book commonly introduced by the verb *confitemur*, "we profess" or "we acknowledge". The Creed in use in the African churches has been reconstructed as follows:

We believe in God the Father Almighty, the Creator of the universe,

    the King of the ages, immortal and invisible:
We believe also in his Son our Lord Jesus Christ,
    born of the Holy Ghost, from Mary the Virgin;
    he was crucified under Pontius Pilate,
    died, and was buried;
    the third day he rose again from the dead;
    he ascended into the heavens;
    he sitteth at the right hand of God the Father;
    from thence he is to come to judge the quick and the dead:
We believe also in the Holy Ghost,
    the remission of sins,
    the resurrection of the flesh,
    eternal life through the Holy Catholic Church.

For the evidence of this and other African creeds see J. N. D. Kelly, *Early Christian Creeds*, pp. 175 ff. A Creed nearly but not precisely the same as this is that commented on in the present work: evidently (§ 56) Augustine's Creed mentioned the Holy Church immediately after the Holy Spirit.

CHAPTER 8

9   At least let hope remain etc.   The poet remonstrates with the gods for sending the portents which precede and presage great catastrophes: if the distresses must come in any case it would be better for us not to suffer from the expectation as well as from the experience of them.

12   If e'er I could have hoped etc.   The speaker is Dido. The writers on the art of composition were, of course, quite wrong. The supreme poet has, with his unfailing felicity, chosen precisely the right word: "If ever I could have foreseen that all my hopes would be thus disappointed, and their only outcome such grief as this"—only he has said it in seven words instead of twenty-two.

37   conviction concerning things not seen.   This discussion might have taken a different form if St Augustine had observed that Hebrews 11. 1 is not intended to be a formal definition of faith but (as the shape of the Greek sentence shows) a concessive description of the kind of faith which was all that the faith of the fathers could be expected to be. The sequence of thought, from the quotation from Habakkuk (Heb. 10. 38) is: "'My righteous one shall have life as a result of faith': we are such as have faith, to the saving of the soul. Now there is a faith which is certainty concerning things hoped for, conviction concerning facts not seen. That this is faith (of a sort) is proved as follows. Without faith it is impossible to please God. Yet it is stated or implied that the fathers did please God: a good report is given of them in the Scriptures. Therefore this conviction on which they acted must have been faith, even if it were only of that very elementary kind which, in the absence of sight, was all that theirs could be. By this faith the fathers did many noble works: but, though they were well reported of for their faith, they had not, as we have, the privilege of sight (11. 1–40). But our faith is fuller than theirs because we can see: we fix our eyes on Jesus, who is the author of our faith (as he was of theirs) but by his actual appearance has made our faith perfect. As then our faith is no longer of that elementary kind, even greater things are expected of us than of them (12. 1–13)." It appears, then, that there is no disagreement between St Paul and his disciple the writer of the Epistle to the Hebrews regarding the nature of faith: it is to both of them the closest of possible personal relationships with Christ, based upon entire surrender to him and trust in him. And of this St Augustine himself was well aware.

CHAPTER 9

Towards the end of the first sentence of the Latin, a comma (not a period) is needed after *existimant*. Augustine is not the only Christian writer who affects to despise secular science and philosophy. Some ancient science was (as Augustine observes) based on *humana coniectura*, mere guess-work, though some of the guesses were surprisingly near the mark: other, by no means to be despised, was derived from *historica experientia*, scientific investigation. It is true enough that sound religion is not necessarily conditioned by such knowledge, and Augustine may have had in mind that many of the attempts to explain natural phenomena and to account for the creation of the world were designed to dispense with the need for a creator and thus to free mankind from religious terrors. Such, for example, was the intention of the great work of Lucretius, *On the Nature of the Universe*: and something of the kind was in Virgil's mind in the famous lines quoted below (§ 16). Augustine's intention was a moral one: it is necessary to know of the Creator's goodness, and his purposes, and " the causes of good things and evil it is our duty to know " (§ 16).

22   existent entity throughout these chapters stands for *natura*, a word which Augustine uses in a special sense. In other writers (e.g. Cicero, *De Natura Deorum*, throughout) *natura* signifies (*a*) genesis or origin: (*b*) those attributes or qualities which characterize an object for what it is (this is the regular meaning of the word in Tertullian): (*c*) the almost personified constructive power behind the world (what in our day is referred to somewhat inaccurately as " evolution "). In Augustine the *natura* is the object itself, the *res*, whether the whole created universe or, more commonly, some particular thing within it. In the chapters which follow, it will be argued that every existent entity, in so far as it is existent and an entity, is good, deriving both its existence and its goodness from the Creator: and that badness is nothing positive, but only a deprivation of natural goodness, a lapse towards non-existence. Thus everything that exists, however bad, possesses at least some residuum of goodness: otherwise it would have totally ceased to exist, and in that case would be neither good nor bad. This explanation of the origin of evil is not peculiar to Augustine: it had been assumed, for example, nearly a hundred years before by Athanasius as part of his argument *On the Incarnation of God the Word*.

25   The clause **and Son,** found only in two MSS., is evidently not part of the text. But Augustine certainly held the doctrine of the " double procession ", in the sense that the Holy Spirit proceeds from the Father *principaliter*, and also proceeds from the Son: see *De Trinitate* xv. 29.

CHAPTER II

The importance of this thesis that all existence, in so far as it is existence, is good, and owes both its being and its goodness to the one Creator, is that it provides a solution of the problem of evil which escapes the moral impasse involved in all dualistic theories, whether Marcionite or Manichaean or gnostic, or any other. For the real problem of evil is not in the long run to explain its existence, or to escape from it, but to abolish it: but if its existence is explained as due either to a creator of its own or to its having been created along with good by the one Creator, it acquires of itself the right to exist, and in that case neither physical nor moral evil can finally be got rid of. It is with moral evil that the Christian is chiefly concerned, and the thesis here set out explains its existence without explaining it away, leaving it possible for the moral problem, by the grace of God, to be capable of solution not in theory only but in actual fact.

11 animate beings, *animalia.* *Anima*, soul, is the life-principle in everything that has life, both animals (including human beings) and plants.

CHAPTER 13

17 Woe unto them etc. Both here and elsewhere, the author's conviction that all Holy Scripture is true in every word and line, leads him to seek to reconcile his conclusions with texts with which at first sight they seem at variance. In the process he often succeeds in bringing out subtle distinctions of meaning, and usually avoids the appearance of straining the sense of Scripture to fit his own ideas. An example of a fruitful conclusion from such a discussion will be found at the end of § 15.

CHAPTER 17

5 one thinks one knows etc. A reminiscence of the famous sophism of Socrates, for which see Plato's *Apology* 6: "So as I went away I reckoned with myself that I was wiser than the man in question: for apparently neither of us knew anything worth knowing, yet whereas he thought he knew when he did not, I neither knew nor thought I knew. Likely enough then I was by this small fraction wiser than he, in not supposing I knew things I was ignorant of." Augustine, however, is not concerned with ironical self-congratulation, or with theories of knowledge, but with the moral danger of the closed mind or of misdirected intention which is the outcome of error in matters of religion. The " things of which ignorance is better than knowledge " which Augustine has in mind are perhaps chiefly idolatrous and magical practices—though there are certain forms of moral disorder against which ignorance is possibly the safest protection, as the apostle says (Rom. 16. 19).

20 an armed band of Donatists. The Donatists made alliance with certain wandering monks (who were in fact no better than sturdy beggars) called *circumcelliones*, and suborned them to attack catholic bishops, and to other deeds of violence. Possidius, in his *Life of Augustine* 12, describes this incident, and indicates that there were other attacks of the same kind, which did not always fail of their purpose.

30 Thus saw I etc. The conclusion of five lines, on the beginning of a boy and girl attachment, which are among the most charming in ancient poetry.

38 Yea, yea etc. What our Lord intends is to forbid the use of any kind of oath to establish a fact: a disciple's bare word ought to be sufficient. But the text is often slightly misquoted, e.g. by Tertullian, *Against Praxeas* 9: "Yea is yea, and nay is nay; for what is more than this is on the side of evil."

43 the very Truth: our Lord himself: cf. John 14. 6.

47 a rational nature. "Nature" still has the sense of "existent entity". The rational natures, i.e. those endowed with reason, are angels and men.

CHAPTER 18

3 The **large book** is entitled *De Mendacio*, and was written apparently in 395. Afterwards, considering the subject

difficult and dangerous, the author tried to withdraw it, but
without success.   A further work, *Contra Mendacium*, was
occasioned by the Priscillianist heretics' contention that for the
purpose of hiding one's religious opinions and escaping
persecution or of insinuating oneself into the good graces of
possible converts, it is permissible sometimes to lie.   See the
Antwerp Benedictine edition, vol. vi, pp. 307, 327, and
Retractations i. 27.   The following sentence refers definitely to
the Priscillianists, and to a book entitled *The Balance* by one
named Dictinius, the theme of which was *ad occultandam
religionem religiosos debere mentiri*, "that it is religious men's
duty to lie, so as to keep their religion a secret".

CHAPTER 19

43   the right road, *ipsam viam*: Bruder, by an obvious
misprint, has *vitam*.

CHAPTER 20

18   The later **Academics** claimed to go back beyond Plato
to the original position of Socrates, but to reject in addition
even his one remaining dogmatism, that he knew he did not
know.   Augustine, who did not read Greek with ease, had
learned of their views from Cicero, who in his philosophical
treatises affects this kind of detachment.   The founder (or
restorer) of the school was Arcesilas (*c.* 276 B.C.): cf. Cicero
Posterior Academics 12. 45: "Arcesilas, in opposition to Zeno
the Stoic, affirmed that it was not possible to know anything,
not even that 'I don't know' which Socrates retained.   He
decreed that all things were hidden and secret, and that nothing
existed which was capable of being perceived or understood.
Therefore no one ought to take the risk of any affirmation or
assent, but always to keep a bridle upon rashness, and guard it
from every lapse: for it would be rashness unbounded if
assent were given in a matter that was false or uncertain.   He
added that there was nothing more sinful (*turpius*) than for
assent and agreement to outrun cognition and perception."
The primary thesis was, of course, that the sense-perceptions
are untrustworthy: the same water feels warm to one hand
and cold to the other, and so forth.   This theme was can-

vassed by Plato, in the *Theaetetus* and elsewhere : and for a
review of several such difficulties, which seem sufficiently
trivial and puerile and admit of an easy answer, see C. E. M.
Joad, *Guide to Philosophy*, Ch. I.   But the true value of the
Academic position was as a protest against the other philo-
sophic schools' practice of quoting the founder's words (*ipse
dixit*) as foreclosing all further discussion and inquiry.   For
this reason, Cicero suggests, it is the other schools which may
be regarded as the true agnostics, for they had shut their
minds to further knowledge : whereas the Academics
reopened the way to further discovery. Cf. Cicero, *De
Natura Deorum* i. 5. 10 ff. : "Indeed, a very great hindrance to
those who desire to learn is the demand made upon their assent
by those who profess to teach : for they cease to make use of
their own judgement, while they regard as beyond question
every statement made by the teacher to whom they have
committed themselves. . . .   Our view, however, is not that
there is no such thing as truth, though we do affirm that
all truths have a certain admixture of falsehood, of so much
verisimilitude that there is in them no certain criterion of
judgement or assent.   From this we conclude that there are
many things which are probable, though our sense-perception
of them is faulty : and yet because they are with a certain
accuracy and clarity present to view, the wise man's life may
well be guided by them."   Also, it must be added, Academic
agnosticism was chiefly concerned with others' theories of the
origin and constitution of the universe : cf. Cicero, op. cit. i.
21. 60 : "As I said before, on almost all subjects, but especially
on natural philosophy, I find it easier to say what my views
are not than what they are."   And we may suppose that
the following sentiment, put into the mouth of a Stoic, was one
with which Cicero had some sympathy : op. cit. ii. 67. 168,
"The practice of arguing against the gods is neither good
morals nor good religion, whether it is done seriously or just
for the sake of discussion".   Augustine's three books *Against
the Academics* are in vol. i of the Benedictine edition.

38 **the happy life,** *vita beata*.   This is the expression the
philosophers themselves used.   "Happy" is apparently what

they meant, though the word also implies something of richness and fullness and general satisfaction. In Christian circles, the word took on a higher significance, that of the initial word of the Beatitudes: and, as St Augustine says, "blessedness" of this kind must in the long run involve eternal life.

44 For it is not permissible etc. The reader will observe that Augustine's assumption here is akin to that of Descartes, *cogito ergo sum*. Philosophers subsequent to Descartes have questioned his right to draw this deduction: but after all, one must begin somewhere, and there is a certain rough justice in the words with which Augustine ends this paragraph.

CHAPTER 21

6 Lastly, *postremo*, is the natural word to introduce the final argument of a series. Possibly a few sentences have been lost.

29 be subject to deception. In Bruder's text *tum* has slipped in by mistake.

CHAPTER 22

8 words were appointed, *instituta*. The ancients, both pagan and Christian, regarded speech not as a product of human evolution but as a divine gift: cf. the interpolated verse at Ecclus. 17. 5.

12 And the fact etc. Bruder misprints *nullum* for *ullum*.

38 in this mortal life, *in hac mortalitate*. *Mortalitas* in Cicero means the fact of being subject to death: another meaning of the word is "epidemic" or "pestilence".

CHAPTER 23

10 falls short. But *deficere*, especially when predicated of *voluntas*, means a purposeful defection rather than an accidental failure.

CHAPTER 24

This chapter summarizes in few words the Christian theory of the origin of evil. It will be observed once more that Augustine treats the whole problem as a moral one. Cf. *Confessions* vii. 12: "It became clear to me that things in process of corruption are good things. If they were in the highest sense good, they would not be capable of corruption: neither could they suffer corruption if they were no good at all. For if they were good in the highest sense, they would be incorruptible; while if they were no good at all, there would be nothing in them to be corrupted. For corruption is a species of injury: and unless it were causing a diminishing of goodness, there would be no injury. Either then corruption does no injury (which is impossible), or else (and this is beyond question) all things in process of corruption are being deprived of goodness. If, however, they are deprived of all goodness, they will cease to exist. For should they continue to exist, while incapable of further corruption, they will be better than they used to be, because they will be continuing for ever in incorruptibility. And what is more absurd than to allege that their condition has improved by their having lost all their goodness? So then, if they are deprived of all their goodness, they will cease to exist: and consequently, so long as they do exist, they are good things. Thus all things that exist are good things: and that 'evil' whose origin we were looking for is not a substance, since if it were a substance it would be a good thing. For in such a case it would either be an incorruptible substance, a good of the highest kind, or else a corruptible substance: and in the latter case it would have to be good, or it would not be capable of corruption. In this way I perceived, and the fact became clear to me, that thou hast made all things good, and that no substances at all exist which thou hast not made. And although thou hast not made all things of equal value, yet all have their existence because taken one by one they are good, and taken all together are very good, because our God hath made all things 'very good'." Cf. also, to the same effect, *On the Morals of the Manichees* ii. 7. 10 ff.

CHAPTER 25

1 There is a contrast between **its own evils,** those of mankind, and **common evils,** those common to men and fallen angels.

10 **a mirrored image,** *umbra*.

CHAPTER 26

10 **impropriators.** *Possidere* means to take possession of something to which one has no legal right, and *possessores* were "squatters", who (like impropriators) could acquire a certain appearance of right through unchallenged usage.

12 **in that all sinned.** This is the most natural meaning of the Greek of Romans 5. 12, and indeed of the Latin *in quo omnes peccaverunt*: see Sanday and Headlam *ad loc*. Some interpreters of the Latin took *in quo* to mean "in whom", and worked out a theory that the whole human race was so to speak in the loins of Adam when he sinned, and thus shared his sin: cf. a similar argument about Levi, Heb. 7. 9, 10. This was probably not in St Paul's mind: nor for that matter is it in St Augustine's. But some doctrine of "original sin", and that not by imitation only, is involved in St Paul's argument. What he seems to mean is what Augustine here develops at greater length, that Adam's sin corrupted his nature, and that that corruption of nature was communicated to his descendants.

CHAPTER 27

1 **The whole lump etc.** The expression *massa damnata* is not so violent as it sounds. The reference is to such texts as 1 Cor. 5. 6 (= Gal. 5. 9), "A little leaven leaveneth the whole lump": and cf. Rom. 11. 16. The "lump" is the dough in the kneading trough. A similar figure is that of the clay ready for the potter's use, for which see Rom. 9. 21.

9 **manifest and apparent.** For *apertis* some MSS. and editions read *opertis*, "secret" or "unapparent". In Bruder's text a colon is needed after *inviti* and a comma after *intercidit*: the comma after *ordinare membra* should be removed.

17 he judged it better.   In the Latin the subject of this sentence is " it ", *sc.* the goodness of God.

22 natural creature (twice), *natura*: see a note on § 9 above.

CHAPTER 28

3 the lower darkness of this air.   In Greek *āēr*, the lower air, as opposed to *aithēr*, the upper air in the region of the stars, was regarded as thick and misty and somewhat opaque.   The Latin writers borrowed the Greek words and the distinction between them.   There was a general suspicion in antiquity, Jewish as well as pagan, that the lower air was inhabited or infested by evil spirits: cf. Eph. 2. 2, and J. A. Robinson's note.

CHAPTER 29

The theory that the purpose of the creation of mankind was the provision of those who should fill the places left vacant in heaven by the revolted angels is not peculiar to Augustine. It is found as early as Tertullian, who speaks of Christians as *angelorum candidati*, " angels designate" (*De Orat.* 3).   It was thought to receive some countenance from Matt. 22. 30 (= Luke 20. 36), " In the resurrection they . . . are as the angels of God in heaven ".   Afterwards it becomes common form, suggesting a large section of the argument of, e.g., Anselm's *Cur Deus Homo?*, and lying behind the prayer in the Burial Service, " that it may please thee . . . shortly to accomplish the number of thine elect ".   There is, however, no suggestion, except in ill-informed circles, that men will be transmuted into angels, but only that, while remaining men, yet clothed upon with immortality, they will occupy the vacant places.

19 our holy mother the Church.   The expression is derived from Gal. 4. 26.   For the history of this idea in Christian devotion see J. C. Plumpe, *Mater Ecclesia* (Washington, D.C., 1943).

K

CHAPTER 30

On the subject of this and the following chapters see the treatises *On the Spirit and the Letter* and *On Nature and Grace*. These, with other of Augustine's anti-Pelagian treatises, and the review of the whole controversy in the Acts of the Second Council of Orange, were edited, with an introduction, by William Bright (Oxford, 1880). Of the two key words, *arbitrium*, "choice", means the power to make a decision between two possible lines of conduct, while *voluntas*, "will" (with its verb *velle*), means the formation of a determination to act, or, in the case of God, the possession of such a determination.

CHAPTER 31

4 obtained mercy etc. What St Paul means at 1 Cor. 7. 25 is that, having no divine command on this particular part of the subject, he gives his own judgement, not with apostolic authority, but as an ordinary Christian, a "believer". But St Augustine's deduction is perfectly legitimate: the faith by which the apostle and others are believers is not of their own making, but is a gift of divine mercy or beneficence. "Mercy" in scriptural language means not merely abstention from punishment, but all the positive expressions of divine goodness besides.

8 For we are his formation etc. The Greek of Eph. 2. 10 means "For we are of his making, founded in Christ Jesus upon the good works which God had prepared beforehand for us to walk in them". But for the more general Greek term *poiēma*, "thing made", Augustine's Latin version had *figmentum*, which recalled the work in clay suggested by the Latin (*de limo terrae*) of Gen. 2. 7. The figure of the potter and the clay is found at Isaiah 29. 16 and 64. 8; referred to at Romans 9. 20, 21: and recurs repeatedly in patristic references to the creation of man.

CHAPTER 32

The subject of this chapter is "prevenient grace". In the course of discussion it was suggested that such people as the

thief on the cross, Cornelius the centurion, and Zacchaeus the
publican, had themselves taken the initiative towards their
own salvation, which initiative was met by the grace of
Christ which saved them. This position, that the first
initiative lies with man, and that God's grace supplements and
perfects it, obtained some adherents at a later stage of the
controversy, after Augustine's death. Augustine had, however, already guarded against it, by his insistence that (even
where the fact is not stated) since there is no evidence to the
contrary, we must assume that God's mercy took the initiative in moving the repentant or the convert to seek for the
further grace of acceptance.

39   His mercy shall anticipate me: Ps. 59. 10, but in the
version given by LXX, and followed by the Latin Vulgate.
According to Driver the Hebrew means, " My God with his
kindness shall come to meet me ", which is precisely the
sense Augustine does not want.

CHAPTER 33

The author's note at the end of this chapter is important.
The expression " the wrath of God " is scriptural, and has to
be taken into account. Human wrath, in its extreme form,
is a soul-shaking and degrading agitation of the kind to which
God is not subject. But, even in human converse, it is
possible, and sometimes necessary, to feel displeasure and to
express disapproval; and this can be done without any
emotional agitation, and consequently without moral harm.
Likewise it is possible to inflict punishment in sorrow rather
than in ferocity. We must take it, our author says, that the
wrath of God, and the vengeance which the Scriptures speak
of, is not degraded by any human agitation or emotion:
but yet that there are things of which God disapproves, and
persons in whom he makes his disapproval plain. The key
phrase, " children of wrath ", must have the meaning Augustine assigns to it: the modern attempt to make it mean
" wrathful children ", as if the estrangement were solely on
our side, is not in accordance with much that St Paul says, both
in Rom. 5 and elsewhere: see J. A. Robinson, *Ephesians*, p. 49.

4 as doth a spider. So the LXX. The Hebrew word is of doubtful meaning, but "spider" is certainly wrong. Driver has "murmur": Kirkpatrick "sigh".

7 He that believeth etc. The speaker is in fact St John the Baptist, unless (as some commentators think) verses 31–36 are a comment by the Evangelist.

17 one and only sacrifice. The doctrine of the Atonement was not in St Augustine's day a matter of controversy. This may be the reason why he seems to pass so lightly over it. That he held the doctrine the present expression places beyond question. See also §§ 49 ff. Perhaps for the same reason he passes lightly over the doctrine of the Holy Spirit and of sacramental grace. It is, however, possible that the importance he attached to the doctrine of predestination tended to throw these other matters into the background: for if there is an absolute predetermination that such and such persons shall be saved by the merits of Christ in baptism, all the rest of the divine scheme of salvation can easily be regarded as various inevitable means of accomplishing a foregone conclusion, and the discussion of *how* they work (granted the fact *that* they work) loses much of its urgency.

18 shadows cast beforehand, *umbrae*: the word could, but probably does not, mean "preliminary sketches". Cf. § 25, "a mirrored image".

CHAPTER 34

On the subject treated in this chapter three points arise. (1) It is a matter of scriptural fact, vouched for explicitly by St Matthew and St Luke, and inferentially elsewhere in the New Testament, that our Lord was virginally conceived through the operation of the Holy Spirit without the agency of any father. The only people known to have denied this were certain Nazarenes or Ebionites in the second century: and by Augustine's day it was beyond all question. (2) A question could arise, and was actually raised about 380 by one Helvidius against whom Jerome wrote an answer: Who were the brethren and sisters of our Lord referred to in the Gospel?

The common belief was that they were either the children of Joseph by a former marriage (which seems most likely) or else were cousins of some sort. Helvidius presumed to suggest that they were subsequent children of Joseph and Mary, thus profoundly shocking pious opinion; for it was commonly assumed that the virginity of Mary was preserved throughout her life. Augustine does not here refer to this question, the answer to it being involved by implication in this third point. (3) A statement was made in the second century in the apocryphal *Protevangelium of James*, where it is supported by embarrassing obstetrical detail, that the outward physical tokens of Mary's virginity remained intact at the nativity as they had not been disturbed at the conception. Clement of Alexandria says that this statement (with which he himself agrees) was unknown to the majority. It was denied by Tertullian, but after his time was apparently everywhere accepted until it was denied by one Jovinian, condemned for heresy at Rome and at Milan in 390. Jovinian in fact propounded a number of anti-ascetical views which were contrary to the ecclesiastical sentiment of the time, e.g. that a virgin is no better than a married wife, that abstinence from meats is no better than to partake of them with thanksgiving, that a person really baptized with the Holy Spirit as well as water cannot sin, that all sins are of equal gravity, and that there is one grade of reward and one grade of punishment in the life to come. Jovinian's denial of the virginal birth (though he did not deny the virginal conception) would seem to arise from the first of these views and not from any *a priori* objection to unauthenticated miracles. Augustine's letter (numbered 137) to Volusianus, referred to at the end of this chapter, was an answer to a series of questions bearing on the Incarnation, the most important being how it could come about that the divine Creator and Sustainer of the universe should be confined (Augustine denies the accuracy of " confined ") within human nature, or should have been in the world without any outstanding and startling effect. On the particular matter of the virginity remaining inviolate at the birth, his answer is to refer to the parallel case of our Lord's emergence from the closed tomb, and his entrance into the upper room when the doors were shut.   A similar answer had been given by Jerome in his reply to Jovinian : and, in spite of one possible objection, that remained the accepted view of a question which probably ought never to have been raised.   See also *City of God* xxii. 8, where an account of what Augustine regarded as a well-authenticated recent miracle closes with the comment : *non credant hoc qui etiam dominum Iesum per integra matris virginalia enixum et ad discipulos ostiis clausis ingressum fuisse non credunt.*

5   so that our faith might be etc.   The words that follow are a quotation from the Creed.   The next sentence, though not from the Creed, has the appearance of being a quotation, perhaps from some prose hymn.   There were a number of such hymns in circulation, though all that have continued in use are *Gloria in excelsis, Te deum laudamus,* and *Quicunque vult.*

8   not by the conversion etc.   Apollinarius, Bishop of Laodicea from A.D. 361, was concerned to maintain the unity of Christ's Person against Diodore of Tarsus, who spoke as if Christ were God in some sort of less than personal union with a Man.   He therefore propounded the untenable theory that in Christ the place of the human soul was occupied by the divine Word.   Either he, or at least some of his sectaries, subsequently held (or were thought to hold) that the whole human nature of Christ was of divine origin, being the substance of the Word converted into flesh.   The theory in both its forms was judged heretical at one of the Councils held at Constantinople, *circa* 380, 381.   Similar views, though not precisely the same, had been held by certain heretics in the second century, the suggestion always being that the flesh of Christ was not of earthly origin nor akin to that of all humanity, but consisted of angelic or perhaps celestial elements transmuted into the appearance of flesh.   For a refutation of several varieties of this view, see Tertullian, *On the Flesh of Christ.*   Such docetism arises as a rule from the idea that there is in human nature something so degraded that God himself cannot escape contamination by association with it, as well as from the desire to be more jealous of God's honour than he is of his own.

9 By "flesh" etc. In Latin (*caro*) and in Greek (*sarx*) the words for "flesh" have a less exclusively material sound than their English equivalent, implying always the existence, either actual or potential, of the animating soul. "Body" (*corpus*, *sōma*) on the other hand is an exclusively material word, at first applied only to dead bodies, and always retaining some sense of inertness and burdensomeness: it is the standing equivalent of the modern scientific term "mass".

10 manhood. The word throughout this discussion is *homo*, which literally means a human person. Latin had no word for "humanity" or "manhood" in the modern attributive or collective sense: *humanitas* meant either "kindness" or the manners of civilized men. So, from Tertullian onwards, all the Latin Christian writers say *homo* for Christ's human nature, unconscious (until the fifth century) of the danger of the Nestorian misconception that at the Incarnation the divine Word associated himself with an independently existent human person. Augustine's language in this and the following chapters shows that he has no fear that anyone will easily fall into such an error: see especially in § 40.

15 bond of sin. "Sin" here is *peccatum*, which means a mistaken or misdirected action: "trespass" later in the sentence is *delictum*, which in legal language means a tort. The difference seems to be that the former word looks at sin in its relation to the doer of it, whereas the latter looks at the loss incurred (or the affront suffered) by the person against whom it is done, namely God.

CHAPTER 35

Once more, at the beginning of this chapter we have what seem to be echoes not of creeds but of devotional or liturgical formulae. The whole chapter should be compared with the decree of the Council of Chalcedon, which (through Leo and his delegates) may have been indirectly influenced by Augustine's language. This itself, as will be observed, is based upon the two outstanding New Testament statements of the Incarnation, John 1. 1-14 and Philippians 2. 5 ff.

CHAPTER 36

The Nestorian misconception, that in Christ the Manhood existed, even in thought or theory, apart from the Godhead, became an urgent matter of debate some few years after this book was written. But it could be read into the treatment of the subject by Diodore of Tarsus (who died about 390) and Theodore of Mopsuestia (died 428). Though these teachers wrote in Greek, Augustine may have been indirectly aware that such ideas were current, and may on that account have seen the necessity of the warning against dualism with which this chapter opens.

3   on this sole occasion, *singulariter*. But the word may conceivably mean " without duality ", though this is implied by " assumed into the unity of the Person ". A few lines lower down the same word evidently means " singularly ", *sc.* to a degree no one else has attained to.

12 the Son of God, the only Son. In Bruder's text transfer the semicolon to follow *unicus*. A few words later, for *propter deum verbum* perhaps read *propter dei verbum*, making the following *quod* more natural.

14 as each and every man etc. Here again either Augustine's language echoes *Quicunque vult*, or that document is based on his words. The analogy here suggested between Word and humanity in Christ, and soul and flesh in any man, is sound enough : but it would probably have been avoided if Apollinarianism had been commonly known of in the West. See above on § 34.

32 full of grace and truth. Augustine, making *plenum* concordant with *verbum*, evidently thinks that this phrase (despite the interposed parenthesis " And we have seen . . . only begotten of the Father ") is attached to the Word who was made flesh. Some modern commentators allege that in biblical Greek the adjective *plērēs* is indeclinable, and so in this instance can be construed with " the Father ". This is doubly wrong, because (1) the word is not indeclinable, occurring eight times in the New Testament in the oblique cases : and (2) the whole point of the sentence is not that the Father is full of grace (any Jew knew that) but that the incarnate Word is. For all that, Augustine is probably mistaken in his further interpretation of the text. He fails to distinguish between the sense in which Mary is full of grace as a recipient, and the other sense in which her Son is full of grace as a donor. Here he was following his Latin Bible, which at Luke 1. 28 had (and still has) *gratia plena*, which represents not very well the Greek *kekharitōmĕnē* : the English Bible somewhat under-translates this by " thou that art highly favoured ". But for this, Augustine might not have been led to distinguish between the Son's manhood as the recipient of grace, and the Only-begotten as possessor of the truth. See, however, Luke 2. 40, " the grace of God was upon him ".

CHAPTER 37

The meaning of the two texts quoted in this chapter evidently is (as Cyril of Alexandria clearly saw : *Comm. in Joannem*, pp. 366a and 993b) that the Holy Spirit is the agent of the miracle of the virginal conception. In connexion with the Incarnation the question of paternity does not arise in any form whatever. Augustine is well aware that any such suggestion is heathenish in the extreme : but he takes far too long to say so.

CHAPTER 38

11 our Creed has it, *confitemur,* the usual formula for quoting from the Creed. But these sentences were certainly not part of any baptismal creed, African or other, and we must suppose that in this case some other statement of faith is meant. The words could conceivably be part of a eucharistic preface.

CHAPTER 41

10 in the old law etc. The sacrifices of the Old Testament were generically of two sorts, thank-offerings and sin-offerings, referred to briefly as " gifts " and " sacrifices " (cf. Hebrews 5. 1). The latter were also described as " concerning sins " or (in the Hebrew) " sins " thus briefly.

Augustine may be right in his interpretation of 2 Cor. 5. 21, though the apostle's language seems to suggest something more than this: as indeed Augustine admits, when he proceeds to quote Romans 8. 3.   See also in § 52 towards the end.

17 He who knew etc.   This false reading can only have originated in Latin copies: in Greek it involves too much alteration.   Even in Latin it is more likely to have been deliberate than accidental, and may have had some antinomian purpose behind it.

The following chapters, 42–53, on the effect of the Atonement as touching human sin, and on the sin which calls for atonement, arise out of the implication contained in the Creed that Christ is the Mediator of God and man.

CHAPTER 44

The illustrations hardly meet the case.   " Sin " is used both in a generic and in a singular sense.   *Miles* in the quotation from Virgil is a collective noun: probably so is " the serpent " in the Hebrew and LXX of Numbers (Latin Vulgate has *serpentes*).   " They " in Matt. 2. 20 either is an indefinite plural or refers to Herod and his familiars.   The Hebrew word for god is a grammatical plural: when it means the true God, it is construed with a singular verb and LXX translates it by the singular: when it refers to false gods, it takes a plural verb in Hebrew, and LXX has the noun as well as the verb in the plural, as in the text here quoted.

CHAPTER 49

3 by the forerunner's ministry etc.   This translation follows the usual interpretation of the text of Isaiah, vouched for by the Gospels.   But Augustine's Latin could more naturally mean, " By a ministry which was a kind of forerunner of him who said, Prepare the way for the Lord ".   In that case the speaker at Isaiah 40. 3 is God the Son commanding the preparation of the way for himself.   Christian writers of the first three centuries assumed almost without question that all the theophanies and divine discourses of the Old

Testament were manifestations of God the Son. Afterwards, apparently owing to the doubtfully orthodox objections of Eusebius of Caesarea, this form of interpretation was dropped, and by St Augustine's day was almost forgotten. In any case he is not likely to have suggested an interpretation in the present case which would be out of harmony with the evangelists', and we may suppose that he has expressed himself with less than his usual clarity.

12   To-day have I begotten thee.   Some texts of Luke 3. 22 (including Codex Bezae) read, "Thou art my beloved Son; to-day have I begotten thee". The reading is found as early as Justin Martyr and Clement of Alexandria, and apparently was in Augustine's copy of the Old Latin.

14   that humanity pertains.   Once more the word is *homo*.

22   the devil, conquered and defeated.   In the New Testament the effect of the Atonement is presented in various forms under the three themes of redemption or deliverance, atonement or reconciliation, and expiation or spiritual cleansing. These must remain the chief heads of the doctrine. Yet there is a further sense in which the atoning work of Christ is a victory over the devil and the powers of evil: see, for example, Colossians 2. 15. As Augustine expresses the idea here, it is beyond cavil: "by truth of righteousness and not by violence of power". But there are other presentations of the case which are not so satisfactory. Gregory of Nyssa suggests that the devil was caught on the hook of Christ's divinity hidden in the bait of his humanity. In answer to this, Gregory of Nazianzus strongly repudiates any idea that the devil was overcome by deception: or that the devil had acquired any rights over mankind for which he could demand payment. Augustine himself, in a sermon (130) and not in a formal treatise, speaks as follows: "And what did our Redeemer do to him who held us captive? To buy us off, he set before him his cross like a mousetrap. He put in it his blood as a sort of bait. The devil had power to shed that blood, but not to drink it. Because he shed the blood of one who was not his debtor, he was ordered to release the debtors. He shed the blood of the innocent, and was ordered to let the guilty go. The Redeemer, in short, shed his own blood so as to wipe out our sins: for the debt by which the devil held us was cancelled by the blood of the Redeemer." Too much emphasis should not be laid upon this single reference to the "mousetrap theory": a popular sermon is not a formal treatise.

CHAPTER 50

6 At Romans 5. 16 the word "offence" is not in the Greek, nor is it in Augustine's Latin. It is supplied by the English translators, and doubtless represents St Paul's meaning.

CHAPTER 51

2 At Romans 5. 18 "judgement passed" and "grace passed" are likewise supplied by the translators.

CHAPTER 52

20 baptized in Christ Jesus. The Greek of Romans 6. 3 requires "into" throughout this passage. Augustine has *in Christo Iesu* and *in morte eius*: but the distinction between accusative and ablative after *in* had become blurred long before his day, and perhaps he meant "into".

27 But to what sin etc. The legitimacy of infant baptism is taken for granted. Even the Pelagians, who denied that infants have any original sin to be forgiven, did not think of challenging the general church practice. Tertullian, a man of many particularities, had objected to what was already in his day established custom: "I know", he says, "that our Lord said, Let the little children come to me: but they can wait and grow up and then come" (*De Baptismo* 18).

41 For in that he died etc. The Benedictine editors, and Bruder, punctuate to make Rom. 6. 10 mean, "For in that he died to sin, he died once for all". This is possible, in Latin as in Greek.

CHAPTER 56

By St Augustine's day it was no longer necessary to argue against the Macedonian suggestion that the Holy Spirit is no more than a kind of very exalted creature. For earlier discussions of the subject see St Hilary of Poitiers, *On the Trinity*; St Basil the Great, *On the Holy Spirit*; and St Gregory of Nazianzus, *Theological Oration V*. St Augustine, *On the Faith and the Creed* 19, has a review of certain outstanding questions, which should be consulted. In our day it is once more necessary to point out that, on scriptural evidence, the Holy Spirit is not merely a divine influence (far less a merely human point of view or a form of human spiritual emotion) but a divine Person.

38 Know ye not etc. The Latin has "your bodies is a temple", which is perfectly good Latin: but the Greek of 1 Cor. 6. 19 has "your body".

CHAPTER 58

By a comparison of certain texts such as those quoted, along with Romans 8. 38, Christian piety first, and the theologians in its wake, worked out a number of ranks or orders of angels. In the liturgy of the *Apostolic Constitutions* viii. 12 (perhaps about A.D. 370) the list is, "Angels, archangels, thrones, lordships, principalities, authorities, powers, armies, ages, cherubim, seraphim". In the fifth-century work *The Heavenly Hierarchy* (falsely ascribed to Dionysius the Areopagite) we have, in descending order, "Cherubim, seraphim, thrones, lordships, powers, authorities, principalities, archangels, angels". Gregory the Great (*Homilies on the Gospels* 34) gives "Seraphim, cherubim, thrones, lordships, principalities, powers, virtues, archangels, angels". This last appears, in the West, to have become the standard list.

18 The question whether the sun and moon and stars are animate bodies was not so foolish to the ancients as it seems to us. Quite reputable philosophers thought that their regular movements proved them to be not only animate but intelligent.   Cf. *City of God* vii. 5 ff., where the opinions of Varro are subjected to criticism.

CHAPTER 59

Augustine, of course, like all theologians of his day and for long after, assumes that all the Old Testament narratives of the appearance of angels among men are literally true.   Tertullian, *De Carne Christi* 6, insists strongly that their bodies were created out of nothing, expressly for the purpose of these visitations, and were afterwards withdrawn into nothingness again.   Once more Augustine is convinced (§ 60) that the moral problem is more important.

CHAPTER 65

The ecclesiastical penitential system varied from province to province, but (for the capital sins of apostasy, adultery, and murder) was everywhere severe.   Not the least part of its severity, as appears from this discussion, was its publicity. Penance had to be done, and remission obtained, by open self-humiliation in the face of the congregation.   One consequence of this was the evil custom of deferring baptism, to give the young time to sow their wild oats : which meant not only that wild oats were sown but also that the young were deprived of the means of grace during the formative period of their lives.   Some English Reformers apparently wished to restore public penance (see the preface to the Commination Service) : fortunately they did not wholly succeed.

CHAPTER 68

St Paul's words at 1 Cor. 3. 12 ff. refer of course primarily to the work of ministers of the gospel like himself and Apollos : though St Augustine may be perfectly justified in his application of them to all Christians, and in the interpretation he gives to them.   Certainly St Paul is not thinking of the fires of purgatory, but rather of the mundane tests to which the minister's work is subjected, and of the degree to which it, and he, survives them.   Augustine, however, was prepared to think (§ 69) that there may conceivably be certain pains of purgation after this life, which may be avoided by present penance. The fuller development of the doctrine of purgatory came later.

CHAPTER 71

3 the right to say Our Father. In the primitive Church the Lord's Prayer was not used in the presence of the unbaptized. The right to call ourselves God's sons comes to us in baptism, in which (by the operation of the Holy Spirit) we are incorporated into the mystical body of the Only-begotten Son, and so are made God's sons by adoption and obtain the privilege of saying " Abba, Father " : Romans 8. 15.

CHAPTER 74

10 having set out etc. Correct Bruder's text : *orationem* for *rationem*.

CHAPTER 75

17 for the rest, give alms. At Luke 11. 41 English R.V. has " Howbeit give for alms those things which are within ", which is just possible as a translation of the Greek. Conceivably the original Syriac for " give alms " was *zakithun*, which could also mean " cleanse ". Thus the sentence would run smoothly. The interpolated sentence, which is probably not by St Augustine, seems to hint at this meaning. Cf. Matt. 23. 26, quoted in paraphrase in § 76.

CHAPTER 78

6 Defraud not one another etc. St Augustine's interpretation of this text is at fault through his failure to remember that *venia* means not only " indulgence " or " pardon " but " permission ". St Paul's meaning at 1 Cor. 7. 6 is that he gives this advice not as an apostolic command, or as defining the law in a matter of morals, but as leaving it to the discretion of the parties concerned to judge what is best. Also his permission is given, or the parties' discretion is allowed, not for the coming together again but for the temporary separation which it is to terminate. Only, he insists, that separation must be by mutual consent, and must not be imposed by one partner upon the other: otherwise that one will be defrauding the other. Tertullian, *Exhortation to Chastity* 3 (and elsewhere), had made the same play with *venia*, with even more disastrous effect.

CHAPTER 80

19 I was expounding etc. See the *Exposition of Galatians* 35. The intention of St Paul, Augustine says there, was in the first instance to deprecate Christians' observance of Jewish fasts and festivals. Nowadays, he adds, if any one sees a convert from Judaism keeping the sabbath, the congregation is in an uproar. Yet the same people who object to this are the first to frequent soothsayers and "mathematicians" to inquire for propitious days on which to start a building or begin a journey. They will boldly tell you, " Of course I'm not setting out on the second of the month ", and the superstition is so common that one can do no more than smile, for fear of being taken for someone peculiar. " Woe to the sins of men etc."

CHAPTER 82

9 Lest peradventure etc. This is a literally correct translation of the Greek, but evidently in its own context makes nonsense. St Paul, according to a later Greek use, has written *mēpŏtĕ* for *eipŏtĕ*, which would mean " If peradventure ". The Latin ought to have not *ne forte* but *si forte*. Repentance is a process, rather than a single act. It begins with conviction of sin, and passes on to contrition and confession: which, being met by the divine grace of forgiveness and the further grace of perseverance, results in amendment of life. The whole process, in its beginning as in its ending, is a God-given grace, in fact, an act of God. St Augustine, with the primitive Church generally, associated this spiritual process with the performance of public penance and the grant of ecclesiastical absolution. *Respexit*, in the Latin of Luke 22. 61, could be taken to mean " had respect unto ", as well as " looked upon ".

CHAPTER 83

The book referred to seems to be *Sermon* 71, which is long
enough to be considered a short treatise. The question, St
Augustine says, is the most difficult in Holy Scripture, and
therefore he has always hitherto avoided preaching on it. Put
briefly, his conclusion is that the sin against the Holy Spirit is
impenitence and despair and schism.

CHAPTER 84

Some of the questions discussed in the following chapters
seem sufficiently remote from modern ideas of reality. They
were apparently at that date of some urgency, being treated
of in similar terms but at greater length in *City of God* xxii.
8–21. We now know, as the ancients did not, that the whole
physical composition of each human body changes every seven
years, while yet each body retains its own characteristics, even
such acquired ones as the scar of an old wound. It is therefore possible for the body to remain the same body, while not
retaining the same physical elements: and this fact may have
some bearing on the resurrection. The essential point is that
the Christian doctrine is not just of the immortality of the
soul, but of the resurrection of the body, the whole person
being reconstituted again for enjoyment of the life to come.
The earliest Christian treatise on the resurrection is by
Athenagoras of Athens (*circa* 180): Tertullian wrote on the
same subject. Athenagoras discusses several difficulties which
have a fairly modern sound. But for the most part the only
Christians of that age who denied a physical resurrection
were those who, being tainted with Marcionism, Gnosticism,
or Manichaeism, regarded everything material as essentially
and irretrievably evil and as unworthy of God's interest and
acceptance.

CHAPTER 85

3   of being born again: *sc.* in baptism.

CHAPTER 87

5 St Augustine refers to this twin in *City of God* xvi. 6. A similar pair was born in Calabria in 1831, both girls: and another pair in Siam, also girls, about 1890.

CHAPTER 91

St Paul's statement "It is sown a natural body; it is raised a spiritual body" must be taken in conjunction with what he says earlier in the epistle (1 Cor. 2. 6 ff.) about the carnal man, the natural man, and the spiritual man. Every man is constituted of the three elements, body, soul, and spirit, and takes his character from that of these which he allows to be predominant. The body is the material element, and the carnal man at his worst is the sensualist, while at his best he might be the athlete, if the athlete were nothing more than this. The soul is the natural life-principle in men and animals or even plants. There being in English no adjective derived from "soul", the English Bible says "natural man": in Latin the word is *animalis*, which is translated in this chapter by "animate". The "natural man" at his best is the scholar or philosopher who is making the highest use of his natural faculties, but does no more than that. The "spirit" is that in our human constitution through which we come into relationship with God, and upon which the grace of God works without intermediary: and the "spiritual man" is he in whose life and character this is the leading principle. Cf. Augustine, *On the Faith and the Creed* 23: "There are three constituents of human nature, spirit, soul, and body. These are occasionally collected into two, because soul is often conjoined with spirit, seeing that the rational part of the soul, which the beasts have not, is designated 'spirit'. So our highest faculty is spirit: after that the life wherewith we are conjoined to the body is called 'soul': and in the last place, the body, because it is visible, is our lowest element. . . . Spirit is also referred to as 'mind' . . . and the soul, while it still hankers after fleshly goods, is called 'the flesh'. . . . The soul's nature is most perfect when it is subject to its own spirit, and follows it as it too follows God (*sequitur sequentem deum*)." Consequently, as concerns this life and the next: the body now is a " natural " or " animal " body, because it is ruled by or through the soul (*anima*): after the resurrection it will be a " spiritual body ", not because it will have been transmuted into spirit, but because it will be directly under the spirit's control. This is what St Paul means, and what St Augustine here repeats.

23   intermediary, *sustentaculum*, prop or support.

CHAPTER 92

3   by man at the first, *per hominem primum*. The meaning may be " the first man ", though for this *per primum hominem* would be more natural.

CHAPTER 93

This chapter is evidently concerned only with the un-baptized.

CHAPTER 94

The discussion of predestination and kindred subjects contained in chapters 94–107 arises in connexion with the resurrection and the life of the world to come because it will be in the full view of the presence of God that the perfect justice will be seen and appreciated of facts which here seem to be " not quite fair ". The question of God's foreknowledge, and of the ultimate irresistibility of the divine will, had been raised: indeed the former is so obvious a question that it was bound to be raised. Whether St Augustine has given the right answers may perhaps be open to discussion: it is possible that, but for the exigencies of controversy, he might have taken refuge at an earlier stage in an attitude of discreet agnosticism. But it was not possible for him to repudiate St Paul (in the texts quoted) or St Peter (Acts 2. 23; 1 Peter 1. 2; cf. Acts 4. 28). Moreover this is not specifically a Christian or even a religious problem. It is bound to arise in any philosophy not based upon atomic physics and behaviourist morals. So if St Augustine finds himself constrained at the same time to safeguard the effective operation of the divine will and the freedom of man's will with its concurrent responsibility, he is discussing a Christian (or theistic) application of a more general problem. And if he seems, while doing less than justice to the human element, to say things which to our present view are inconsistent with human conceptions of divine righteousness, he takes refuge beforehand in the thought that some time all will be made clear. For the vision of God solves all problems.

CHAPTER 99

18 had compacted, *concreaverat* : an otherwise unknown word, apparently a causative of *concresco*.

CHAPTER 100

19 contrary to . . . in spite of: *contra . . . praeter.*

CHAPTER 103

11 request should be made etc. Here again St Augustine is unable to repudiate St Paul, who enjoins that all men should be prayed for. Yet there is an obvious superficial inconsistency with the main argument : for if all things are predestinate and foreknown, it might be supposed that the will of God is already fixed, and Christians could but follow the Roman poet's advice, *desine fata deum flecti sperare precando.* The inconsistency is admitted. It might have been thought that, in view of the Calvinism which has reigned there for three centuries, Scotland would be a country in which no prayers would be said and no effort would be made : yet it is doubtful if there has ever been so generally prayerful and industrious a nation. Possibly this question, like that of Achilles and the tortoise, *solvitur ambulando.*

CHAPTER 106

10 for any man can make etc. In Bruder's text close the parenthesis after *occidere*, not after *desint*.

23 as it is written etc. Prov. 8. 35, " and shall obtain favour of the Lord ", appears in LXX as " and the will is prepared by the Lord ".

CHAPTER 107

3 the wages etc. At Rom. 6. 23 St Paul perhaps had in his mind the distinction between the Roman soldier's pay (*stipendium*, Greek *opsōnia*) which was his due, and the occasional *donativum* (Greek *charisma*, here and in the Vulgate translated by *gratia*) which was a free and unearned bounty from the Emperor or the general in command.

CHAPTER 108

If we have had cause to remark (see above on § 33) that St Augustine speeds lightly over the doctrine of the Atonement, the present chapter is sufficient evidence that it is present to his mind, and so strongly present that, even if not discussed formally, it is the standing background of his faith, and must be repeatedly referred to.   Yet again, this summary is homiletic rather than doctrinal : and it is no bad thing that the central mystery of the Faith should be more a matter of devotion than of argument.

CHAPTER 110

On the ancient Christian practice of making prayers and offering the eucharist for the dead see Bingham's *Antiquities* XV. iii. 16–18 and XXIII. iii. 12, 13.   The only people known to have objected to the custom are a certain Aerius and his rather numerous followers in Armenia *circa* 350 : see Epiphanius, *Haereses* 75, and Augustine (who draws all his information from Epiphanius), *De Haeresibus* 53.   The practice existed in Tertullian's day, and by the fourth century was universal.   Augustine felt bound to accept and approve of the church custom, but with this difference, that whereas the church prayers were on behalf of all deceased Christians without distinction, Augustine suggests that they are actually beneficial only to the not perfectly good, while in respect of the saints and martyrs they are a thanksgiving, and in respect of the very bad they are no more than a consolation to the survivors.   In the West this view eventually prevailed, and at Rome some slight but significant changes were made in the church service to avoid the appearance of praying for the saints.

2 deceased: *defuncti* really means "those who have completed their task".

14 merit or demerit, *meritum*, which (as the context shows) means both these.

16 So let no man etc. The variant text recorded here by the Benedictines and Bruder will construe, but makes no sense.

CHAPTER 112

The questions summarily answered in this and the following chapter are discussed at greater length in *City of God* xxi.

19 one would need to surmise etc. In Bruder's text the comma after *finem* must be removed.

CHAPTER 113

6 the easing: read *relevatione*.

CHAPTER 114

Having completed his discussion of the Faith, St Augustine ends his book with a short account of hope and charity. These are so closely associated that the references to them are interlaced. Prayer, for example, is a matter of hope when it concerns oneself, and of charity when it concerns others.

CHAPTER 115

The ancients tended to deprecate the composing or extemporizing of private prayers. Except for the church prayers the general suggestion was that the Lord's Prayer should be said thrice a day: cf., e.g., *The Teaching of the Twelve Apostles* 8 (but this book is of no more than private authority). There are fuller explanations of the Lord's Prayer by Tertullian (who adds a supplementary list of things that may rightly be prayed for and of other prayers, such as psalms and ejaculations, which may rightly be said) and St Cyprian (who had Tertullian's work before him). St

Cyril of Jerusalem and the author (possibly St Ambrose) of the
Ambrosian *De Sacramentis* comment on the Lord's Prayer in
the course of their explanation of the eucharistic canon. From
Tertullian comes the interpretation " in the spirit and in the
body ". The comparison between St Matthew's and St
Luke's version of the Prayer is apparently St Augustine's own.

CHAPTER 116

Both the longer and the shorter versions of the Prayer at
Luke 11. 2–4 are ancient : but the authorities for the longer
version are not as a rule older than the end of the fourth
century. See the apparatus criticus in Souter's Greek
Testament.

CHAPTER 117

Towards the end of this chapter there are three pairs of
assonances, *impetrat, imperat* : *iubere, iuvare* : *caritas, cupiditas* :
which I have attempted to reproduce by " on demand ",
" as a command " : " command ", " commend " (not very
successful) : " charity ", " cupidity ".

CHAPTER 118

38 the ancient righteous men etc. See a curious argument in Augustine's *De Catechizandis Rudibus* 6, which
reaches the unexceptionable conclusion : " So although our
Lord Jesus Christ sent before him a part of his body (*sc.* his
mystical body) in the saints who were born before his coming,
yet is he the head of the body, the Church, and all those (*sc.*
patriarchs and prophets) were in union with that same body of
which he is the head, seeing they believed in him whom they
were announcing beforehand. For they were not torn off
from it by being his forerunners, but rather were united with
it by being his followers." Such language finds scriptural
justification in John 8. 56 ; 1 Cor. 10. 1–4 ; and elsewhere.
Christian writers until the fourth century went further : they
assumed as beyond question that it is God the Son who is the
God of revelation, and that it was he in his own Person who

appeared in visions and theophanies to the patriarchs and
prophets.

CHAPTER 119

6   The Spirit bloweth etc.   At John 3. 8 "spirit" at the
beginning of the sentence means the wind : later it means the
Holy Spirit.   Augustine apparently thinks it means the Holy
Spirit both times.

CHAPTER 120

This paragraph seems to mean that every man begins (even
if it be for the few days or hours before his baptism as an
infant) by living after the flesh, and that it is to this period of
his life that the commandment is addressed.   Baptism is the
first and final step towards the keeping of the commandment,
because in it the grace of God is given.   If then a person dies
immediately after baptism, without having had time to be
practised in the commandment, he loses nothing of final
perfection, for the grace of baptism gives him all he needs.

CHAPTER 121

30   until charity attain.   Evidently read *haec* for the
manuscripts' and editors' *hic*, which makes no sense as either
adverb or pronoun.

36   contention from death, *contentio mortis.*   At 1 Cor.
15. 55 the later form *nikŏs* is written for *nīkē* (victory).   This
was misread as *neikŏs*, "quarrel" or "contention".   Latin
Vulgate has *victoria*.

INDEX OF SCRIPTURAL REFERENCES

IN THE TEXT

The figures on the right refer to the smaller chapter divisions of the text.

IN THE INTRODUCTION AND NOTES

The figures on the right refer to pages of this edition.

INDEX TO OTHER ANCIENT AUTHORS

References are to pages of this edition.

145